Waterfalls
of the
Blue Ridge

Waterfalls of the Blue Ridge

by Nicole Blouin,
Steve Bordonaro, and
Marilou Wier Bordinaro

MENASHA RIDGE PRESS
BIRMINGHAM, ALABAMA

Printed in the United States of America
Published by Menasha Ridge Press
First Edition

Blouin, Nicole, 1966-
    Waterfalls of the Blue Ridge/by Niclole Blouin and Steve & Marilou Bordonaro
        p.   cm.
    Includes index.
    ISBN 0-89732-128-6 : $14.95
    1. Hiking -- Blue Ridge Parkway (N.C. and Va.) --Guidebooks.
2. Trails --Blue Ridge Parkway (N.C. and Va.) --Guidebooks.
3. Waterfalls --Virginia -- Guidebooks. 4. Waterfalls --North Carolina --
-Guidebooks. 5. Blue Ridge Parkway (N.C. and Va.) -- Guidebooks.
I. Bordonaro. Steve. 1951 -   . II. Bordonaro, Marilou. 1950 - .
III. Title.
GV 199. 42. B65B56   1994
796.5 '1'09755--dc20   94-11052
                                                                         CIP

Frontispiece photo of Looking Glass Falls by Ben Keys

Menasha Ridge Press
3169 Cahaba Heights Road
Birmingham, Alabama

Dedication

For my grandfather, Jack A. Blouin. In this way, I can share something of my world—waterfalls and the Blue Ridge Mountains.

—Nicole

To Megan (age 10) and Cory (age 8), our heart and soul. May your paths be long and happy and always lead to the waterfalls.

—Steve and Marilou

Rainbow at the base of Dry Falls, North Carolina. Photo by John Newman.

Acknowledgments

I would like to give credit to those who made this book possible. My role as an author was primarily to tie together the contributions of the many people who were involved in the research, the field work, and the writing. Any merit from this project is due in part to those mentioned in the following.

While I researched, I drew on the expertise of individuals from chambers of commerce, the park service, the forest service, and other agencies and organizations. Their cooperation immensely added to the depth of this work. I would like to highlight a few of these people.

I express appreciation to Janet Stombock, Chief Interpreter at Shenandoah National Park; William Knick, Town Manager of Glasgow; Lee Thompson, a ranger in the Toecane District of Pisgah National Forest; Jerry Delaughter, from the Burnsville Chamber of Commerce; and Mary Virginia Adams, whose family once owned Catawba Falls.

Also, Tom Wagoner (Hanging Rock State Park), Jim Billings and Larry Tribute (Stone Mountain State Park), and Walt Gravely (South Mountains State Park) made significant contributions. Thank you for answering questions, checking my facts, and supplying photographs.

During the year I worked on the book, I enjoyed the field work the best—walking and exploring in the woods. Mostly, I hiked alone, but my fondest memories are of the trips that I shared with friends. Thank you for spending the day with me Betina, Nancy, Leonard, and Amy Jo. In particular, I'd like to thank Mom and Dad for the morning walk on the Glen Burney Trail and lunch at the Speckled Trout Cafe; and Victoria, Frank, and Griffin Logue for joining me on the last hike of the project—Fallingwater Cascades.

Even when I wrote, I was not alone. The paragraphs about the base towns or state parks for seven of my fifteen chapters were prepared by writers other than myself. The manuscript would not have met the publisher's deadline without their contributions. I am immensely grateful to: Dave Arkoette for Stone Mountain State Park; Bob Beazley for Hanging Rock State Park; Jennifer Emerson for Marion; Bill Hester for Wilson Creek, which didn't get included; Rebecca Jacobson for Linville; Katie McNamara for Blowing Rock; and Donna Obrect for Asheville. Good luck and happiness in all your writing pursuits.

Also during the writing phase, I "re-wrote" based on the suggestions provided by my friendly (and free!) unofficial editors. Special thanks to Sue McNamara, Budd Zehmer, Betina George, Phil Fairbrother, Ellyn Fienroth, and Brenda Blouin for reading early drafts and furnishing helpful comments.

So many people assisted me throughout all the phases of this project that I must depart from paragraph form and begin listing. Thanks to:

➤Leslie Cummins, who was instrumental as more than just my editor, for answers to questions from A-Z, and for humor.

➤Frank Logue for the book design.

➤Beth Maynard, appreciated first as a friend and second as my photography mentor, for her invaluable knowledge and encouragement.

➤Tom Vargo for the nature photography workshop, in which, to my surprise, the nature turned out to be waterfalls.

➤Photographers Don Wacker, John Newman and Ben Keys for their willingness to supply slides for the book.

➤Stu Smiley and Steve McWhirt, my employers at Wildwater Ltd., and Dave Perrin and Ellyn Fienroth, my employers at the Nantahala Outdoor Center, for giving me work when I wanted it, as well as days off when I needed it.

➤Jack Wise and Frank Logue, without whose computer expertise I might have lost the entire manuscript.

➤Lisa Johnson for her diligence in typing those last five chapters into WordPerfect.

➤Ross and Eleanor Howell for supplying hospitality, great food, and friendship during the cold and wet (and snowy!) trip to Virginia. And Carolyn and Alton Sakowski for the place to crash in Winston-Salem, and the local lore.

➤Cory and Megan for, without complaint, letting me have the full attention of their parents while we worked.

As always, the best for last. My co-authors, Steve and Marilou, how can I express my gratitude? I am indebted to you for your hard work, your patience, and most importantly, your vision. Best of everything, always. And finally, to my husband, Mike, for making so many things possible, including my first book.

–Nicole Blouin

A project of this magnitude required the assistance of people too numerous to mention. There are a few, however, whose help proved invaluable, and to whom we wish to express our appreciation. Thanks to:

➤Jim Bob and Dottie Tinsley for leading us to the waterfalls and inspiring us to "keep on trekking."

➤Skip Dunn for leading us to the Tinsleys.

➤Jack Hall of the Lake Toxaway Company for his valuable input and his generous gift of time.

➤Sue Elderkin and Don Dyer of the U.S. Forest Service, Pisgah District of the Pisgah National Forest, for their facts and directions.

➤Patricia and Clark Grosvenor of the Key Falls Inn for their gracious hospitality, and Beth Womble of the Womble Inn for hers.

➤Esther Wesley of the Brevard Chamber of Commerce for her guidance, Tim and Peg Hansen of Highland Books in Brevard for their resources and assistance, John Barbour of the Nantahala Outdoor Center for his input.

We would also like to thank our parents, Tommy and Marianne Wier, as well as Laura, Jerry, and Jennifer Jackson, for entertaining Megan and Cory those many weekends we were working on the book. And thanks to Megan and Cory, who have shared a lot of our explorations and who have displayed patience far beyond their years.

Finally, thanks to Nicole Blouin and Michael Jones for allowing us to be involved in this project. It opened our eyes to our own "backyard."

–Steve and Marilou Bordonaro

The bottom drop on Whitewater Falls. Photo by Nicole Blouin.

Table of Contents

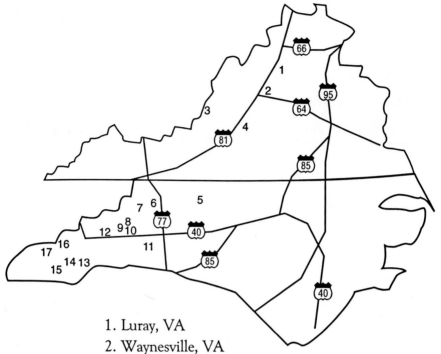

1. Luray, VA
2. Waynesville, VA
3. Clifton Forge, VA
4. Glasgow, VA
5. Hanging Rock State Park, NC
6. Stone Mountain State Park, NC
7. Blowing Rock, NC
8. Linville, NC
9. Little Switzerland, NC
10. Marion, NC
11. South Mountains State Park, NC
12. Asheville, NC
13. Transylvania County, NC
    Including Brevard, Pisgah Forest and
    Lake Toxaway
14. Cashiers, NC

Introduction

Waterfalls are perhaps nature's most captivating wonder. They are magical, holding all the secrets of the woods. Although it seems simple—falling water—we are astonished at finding one of these moving spectacles hidden within the folds of the forest.

Mountain streams leave their birthplace, stretching and rushing towards the sea. They are fed by springs and rains as they travel down ancient slopes following channels carved out years before. Reaching an edge, they fall, creating an enchanting place to become lost in time and space.

For some people, waterfalls are simply an excellent place to picnic. For others, waterfalls are the center of all wild places. Whichever the case, waterfalls make you feel good. They are therapeutic. Some scientists believe this is because of the negative ions they produce, similar to a "cozy-glowing-toasty" fire, the endless rolling of the ocean surf, or a thunderstorm.

Remember when you were a kid and you'd plan your attack on an OREO cookie. You'd twist the chocolate wafer apart and dig your teeth into the filling until the cream surface looked like tire tracks in the snow. The chocolate wafer could stand alone, but the cream filling is a special treat. The same can be said about walking in the woods and discovering a waterfall. A hike could stand alone, but it is even better when combined with the chance to visit a waterfall.

Waterfall trekking in the mountains of the Blue Ridge is a marvelous way to experience the outdoors. Trails to waterfalls lead through national forests and national parks, through state and city parks, and even through private and commercial properties.

You can seek out a different waterfall every time or hike to a favorite falls over and over. During an early morning walk, you might catch a glimpse of a wild animal drinking from his water hole below the falls. Camp beside a waterfall and fall asleep to the sound of rushing water.

Waterfalls have interesting names. Some falls have more than one name. Carter Creek Falls is also called Douglas Falls. Others share common names, such as Upper Falls or the Cascades. Silver Run Falls has a beautiful name, Blue Suck Falls has an unusual name. The name Widow's Creek Falls makes you curious. Like many waterfalls, Soco Falls and Lower Cullasaja Falls get their names from Indian words.

Visiting one waterfall is not the same as visiting them all. They are all different, taking on many shapes and many forms. A waterfall might free-fall off a sheer drop or cascade down a slide. A waterfall might flow over several drops in a row, or plunge into a pool and then plunge again, creating individual waterfalls.

Each waterfall has its own personality. Some are exceptional for the water volume they command; others, for the tremendous height from which they fall. Grand or gorgeous or graceful, bubbling brook or roaring river, we've never met a waterfall we didn't like.

The personality of a waterfall changes with each rainfall. Rain saturates the ground and fuels the creeks and rivers. Falls swell with an abundance of water—a delicate cascade might become a raging waterfall on the next visit, and vice versa.

The personality of a waterfall also changes with every season. The colors reflected in the clear mountain water shift from pastels and greens to shades of autumn and earth tones. As months fall off the calendar, foliage around the falls blooms and flourishes and withers away. The weather turns from warm to hot, from cool to cold. At one time of the year, a flower grows out of a crack in the rock, watered by the constant spray of the falls; at another time of the year, an icicle hangs in its place.

Visit a waterfall in the spring and you'll see a pink-and-purple procession of flowering mountain laurel and rhododendron. Waterfalls overflow from April rains, which bring May wildflowers to blanket the earth. The hillsides cry out for a wedding.

Visit a waterfall in the summer and you'll enjoy the cool mist that drifts lazily off the face of the falls. This time of year, you can allow the waterfall to absorb you. Sink into the swimming hole at the base of the falls, lean back, and let the water from above cascade over you. Relax and restore your soul.

Visit a waterfall in the fall and you'll be surrounded by the brilliant reds, yellows, and oranges of the hardwood forest. Color frames the white frothy cascade, painted leaves swirl and dance on the surface of the clear stream. Lie on a warm rock and bask in the sun for awhile. The Indian summer days of autumn, with crisp air and cloudless skies, send an irresistible invitation for an adventure in the woods.

Visit a waterfall in the winter and you'll experience a subdued wilderness and wonderful solitude. Formations of ice create picturesque sculptures, dangling from rocky cliffs. The snow-covered ground brings a stillness to the forest, the bare trees open up unobstructed views. There is beauty in a colorless scene--white on gray and brown.

The hills of the Blue Ridge harbor an incredible number of waterfalls. Visitors, and even locals, are usually unaware of how many extraordinary cascades adorn the area. The waterfall collector will find heaven in the mountains of North Carolina and Virginia, where hundreds of "named" waterfalls, and thousands of others, are waiting to be discovered.

Welcome to the waterfalls of the Blue Ridge!

1

How to Use This Book

This book is a collection of approximately one hundred waterfalls in the Blue Ridge, found along seventy-five trails. The waterfalls range in height from ten feet to five hundred feet, the trails range in length from "no hike required" to ten miles roundtrip.

For the purpose of this book, we defined the Blue Ridge as the mountainous region along the Blue Ridge Parkway between Great Smoky Mountains National Park and Shenandoah National Park. *Waterfalls of the Blue Ridge* will take you to two states, Virginia and North Carolina; four national forests, George Washington, Jefferson, Pisgah, and Nantahala; three national parks, Shenandoah, Blue Ridge Parkway, and Great Smoky Mountains; six state parks, Douthat, Hanging Rock, Stone Mountain, Mt. Mitchell, South Mountains, and Ceasar's Head (South Carolina); two wilderness areas, St. Mary's and Linville Gorge; and the Cherokee Indian Reservation. To the list, add a city park, a country club, and several tracts of private land.

The waterfalls are grouped together according to their proximity to a particular town or their location in a state park. We call these "base towns," and the book contains twenty. Each chapter describes a different base town in North Carolina or Virginia, followed by details on several waterfalls that are within approximately a fifteen-mile radius. (Driving distances between a waterfall and its base town range from 0.5 to 30 miles.)

Planning Your Trek

To arrange a day of waterfall trekking, look under the chapter for the base town you plan to visit. Using the information provided, you can plan hikes that fit your time limitations and physical ability. Choose a waterfall trail where you can spend the whole afternoon or chart out a circuit and visit several in one day. We've provided trail distances and difficulty, waterfall descriptions, and general directions.

Trail Distance

The mileage listed for each hike is recorded as the total distance—roundtrip (there and back) or a loop. A pedometer, a simple instrument that hooks to your waist and calculates mileage by stride length, was used when accurate trail length wasn't posted or otherwise available. All mileage is specified to the nearest one tenth.

If you are not good at judging distance, we suggest that you purchase a pedometer. This gadget will prove useful when you want to know "How much farther is it?" The pedometer can be fairly reliable if used correctly.

To estimate how long it will take you to hike a certain distance, take into account your hiking style, physical condition, and trail conditions, and figure that the "average" hiker covers about two miles per hour.

Trail Difficulty

The ratings for trail difficulty are based on the amount of energy expended by an average, healthy person. More effort is needed for each level—easy, moderate, and strenuous. Trail difficulty really means elevation gained per mile. The longer and steeper the grade, the more difficult the trail.

Easy. It is possible to hike an easy trail without getting tired. The gradient is generally flat with slight inclines.

Moderate. You may be somewhat winded and need an occasional rest on a moderate hike. The trail will have some modest inclines.

Strenuous. The average hiker will definitely feel the work-out on a strenuous trail. Several breaks may be necessary. The trail will have steep sections.

Waterfall Descriptions

Waterfalls are always being described by superlatives: the highest...the widest...the most. Most of the waterfall descriptions we have read use an amazing stack of adjectives that don't truly express the character of the falls.

In order to be more informative, we tried to use as many specifics as possible. Each waterfall description gives an estimated height of the falls and some brief details. Other specifics include width, number of tiers, average flow, and angle of the falling water.

Most people prefer a waterfall with lots of volume. Some waterfalls are always powerful, others fluctuate dramatically with rainfall. If you want to see a waterfall at its "best," watch the weather. Sometimes it just takes one good thunderstorm. But remember, the beauty of a waterfall is not necessarily tied to its rate of flow.

Directions

The most frustrating part of this project was getting lost. We got so lost, so many times! Finding a waterfall can be difficult, but that's part of the adventure—right? It would take pages to describe every mile of road and every foot of trail, but we did our best to make our directions as clear as possible to help you stay "found."

Detailed driving directions, positioned at the end of each waterfall entry, will get you to the trailhead. The location of a trailhead is always indicated. (For example: "at the upper end of the parking area" or "just past the red gate on the left.") General trail information, positioned within the waterfall entry, will get you to the waterfall.

On the road, be aware that street signs change and new roads alter routes. On the trail, don't rely completely on blazes or markers, which are susceptible to vandalism. On private land, keep in mind that a land owner who allowed access in the past may choose not to let you onto his property. "No trespassing" signs must be respected.

To find out more about a waterfall, a trail, or an area, go to the back of the book. The appendix lists an address and phone number for every base town, either a local chamber of commerce or a state park headquarters. We also included information needed to contact Shenandoah

National Park, Great Smoky Mountains National Park, and the Blue
Ridge Parkway.

Visiting Waterfalls

The rest of this chapter is devoted to minimal impact techniques, safety
and photography. The first two are an extremely important part of any
hiking guide. We must hike smart and hike green. The third—waterfall
photography—was included for fun. Based on our experience and the
experience of others, we offer a few tips to help you capture the beauty
of a waterfall on film.

Wilderness Ethics and Etiquette

More and more hikers visit the mountains of the Blue Ridge every year.
Waterfall trails are especially popular. The problems are evident: soil
erosion, overcrowding, evidence of others and decreasing numbers of
wildlife and vegetation. Wild places are for solitude and splendor. We
who love wild places must save them.

Stay on maintained trails. You can safeguard against crushing sensitive
plants and increasing soil erosion by not straying from designated paths.
Trail builders strive to create a path which has as little impact on
vegetation as possible, with good erosion control. Do not walk off the
trail, even to avoid muddy stretches, because this destroys the border and
enlarges the trail. The section of trail most often abused is the switchback.
Avoiding the temptation to take a shortcut can save future scars on the
hillside.

Travel quietly in the woods. You are less likely to intrude upon other
hikers, as well as the wildlife, when you walk and talk quietly. Quiet
(earth-tone) colors for clothing and backpacks are more suited to the
wilderness. Move away from the trail when taking a break—your party
and those passing by will benefit.

Hike during the off-season. You help spread out visitor use by taking
advantage of the off-season. Off-season doesn't necessarily mean winter.
Try going on weekdays or very early in the morning.

Travel in small groups. You lessen your impact on other visitors when you're not hiking with a crowd. Large groups cause a disproportionate invasion. A small group is considered fewer than ten people, four to six is even better.

Pack everything out. You can "contribute by not adding." This principle includes biodegradable material. Food scraps are unsightly. If you bury the leftovers, animals will dig them up. Plan ahead—reduce the amount you pack in and carry a bag specifically for packing everything out.

Respect wildlife. You can try to lessen your interruption into their lives. When you enter the wilderness, you are traveling in their home. It is important to not feed the animals. When they become tame, they are no longer wildlife.

Leave the things of nature in their place. You afford others the opportunity to enjoy the same experience that you enjoyed if you do not disturb the natural environment. If every hiker dug up a flower or collected an edible plant, we could quickly deplete an area. Take a photograph of the fire pink and only an occasional sample from the blackberry bush, and you will help protect the vegetation of our backcountry.

We encourage you to do two things. First, adopt one waterfall trail, officially or unofficially, that you can hike at least four times a year. And second, on every waterfall hike, carry a trash bag and spend fifteen minutes picking up after someone else. Let's begin to make a difference— starting with the waterfall trails of the Blue Ridge.

Warnings and Waterfall Safety

Oh no! More rules. That's what we thought. But after talking with forest rangers, park employees, and city officials throughout the Blue Ridge, we discovered that accidents around waterfalls are a serious problem. It is unfortunate that something so lovely can take a life. Crabtree Falls (Virginia) has claimed twenty-one lives to date.

Developed areas can be just as dangerous as undeveloped areas. As one ranger put it, "It is just the nature of rocks and water and cliffs. You can build observation decks and post signs, but people will be careless and use poor judgement."

The hazards are real: waterfalls are dangerous. So, instead of incorporating "a single slip could be your last" into every chapter, we decided to deal with warnings and waterfall safety here. Please, be careful.

➤Stay on developed trails and don't stray from observation points or platforms.

➤Watch your footing. Dry rocks may be slippery, algae-coated rocks are unforgiving.

➤The top of any waterfall is, of course, the most dangerous part. Avoid the temptation to lean over a ledge at the top of the falls.

➤Exercise caution on the trail to the falls, as well as around the falls themselves. Waterfall trails are often treacherous—steep and rocky with sheer embankments.

➤Be especially cautious when taking photographs. You are likely to be paying more attention to your camera than to your footing.

➤Watch children carefully. Children should always be under the immediate supervision of an adult.

➤And watch your dog. My golden retriever, who is sure-footed but doesn't understand the "slick rock" concept, fell off a twelve-foot drop. He was fine, but I almost injured myself trying to get down to him in a hurry.

➤Never hike alone.

As on any day hike, carry a small knapsack or fanny pack with useful items and extra gear. His lordship, Baron Von Mabel, recommends the ten essentials: matches, compass, map, knife, flashlight, sunglasses, fire starter, extra food, extra clothing, and a first aid kit (from *Backpacking* by the late Sheridan Anderson).

Add Ziploc® bags to the list for waterproofing and organizing. And be sure to carry an adequate supply of water. Don't drink any surface water unless it has been boiled for one minute or treated with chemicals.

This list may seem long, but the first six essentials can fit into one Ziploc® bag. Extra food and clothing (a few candy bars and a raincoat/ sweater) don't take up much space. Always keep your day pack filled and ready to go. Check contents occasionally, testing batteries, restocking first aid supplies, and adding to food reserves as necessary.

Photographing Waterfalls

We try to photograph every waterfall we visit. We have a scrapbook that contains our collection. These aren't quality photographs—just snapshots to preserve a memory. Most of the photographs that we've taken of waterfalls aren't great. We've spent a lot of time shooting waterfalls, but getting an excellent shot of a waterfall takes even more time.

You need a tripod. You need slow film. You need early morning or late afternoon light. Capturing the personality of a waterfall may mean several visits, during different times of the year. The photographs in this book are not from our waterfall album. They are the result of two years of hard work, early morning wake-up calls, shooting and re-shooting, and lots and lots of film.

While learning about photography, we have gained some solid insight that relates directly to waterfall photography. We had the good fortune of doing a half-dozen waterfall hikes with a professional photographer. On each walk, we'd watch her work and discover something new. We also read several outdoor photography books and magazines that revealed "secrets" about shooting moving water. Here is a summary of the basics.

Tripod. You'll need a sturdy tripod because you can't hand-hold a camera when using slow shutter speeds. Be sure the tripod is compact and lightweight so you'll be willing to carry it with you no matter how long the hike. Use a cable release, a cord attached to the shutter button that separates you from the camera. This reduces "shake" caused by pressing the shutter button. Twelve inches is a good minimum length for a cable release, and buy a spare because they are easily misplaced. Tripod Rule: Use a tripod whenever you can, especially if the shutter speed is less than the lens focal length. (For example, to hand-hold a 50mm lens, you should use a shutter speed not slower than 1/60 second.)

Film Speed. You need slow film to use slow shutter speeds. Generally, an ISO rating between 25 and 100 is suggested for scenics, although ISO 100 is somewhat fast for waterfalls. These slow films have a fine grain and produce the sharpest images. To see every detail, use the slowest film possible for each particular lighting condition.

Shutter speed. Slow shutter speed gives a sense of movement. Mike

People add perspective to waterfall pictures as this photo of Bridal Veil Falls near Highlands, North Carolina illustrates. Photo by John Newman.

Wyatt, in his book *Basic Essentials of Photography Outdoors*, explains how shutter speed relates to moving current: "The movement of flowing water will be completely stopped at 1/2000 second. The fastest portions of the water will begin to soften at 1/60 second. At 1/15 second, the water's movement will be clearly evident, but the water will not be completely blurred." Most waterfall photographs are shot at 1/8 second or slower to produce a soft and abstract quality.

Time of Day. Mid-day sun creates harsh lighting and black shadows. Visit a waterfall at daybreak or an hour before sunset, and observe the wonderful quality of the light. The light is softer, colors are richer.

Exposure. The white water of a falls will often cause the light meter to underexpose your shot, making the water gray and the foliage slightly dark. You can open up a little and cross your fingers, or you can bracket. Bracketing means shooting at the original reading and increments in each direction (usually half stop increments). If you shoot one "on," two over, and two under, you should get what you want.

Perspective. Waterfall photographs need a reference to indicate their size. To give a feeling of depth and space, use foreground elements, such as trees, rocks, and people. In essence, try to "frame" the waterfall.

Position. Shoot from the top, or the bottom, or the side of the falls, but always try to keep the camera back parallel. Basically, treat the waterfall like a piece of architecture.

People. The high reflectance of water makes your meter want to underexpose people in a waterfall photograph. Open up one to two stops, meter off a grey card or set the exposure by reading only the subject.

Rainbows. If you are lucky enough to find a rainbow at the end of a waterfall, burn a lot of film. Don't miss the opportunity for a spectacular photograph by skimping on film. Underexpose slightly to increase the color saturation—bracket one to two stops.

Things to Watch For. Watch the sun. Light reflecting in the lens between the glass surfaces can cause a "flare" (diffused spot) or a "ghost" (multi-sided bright spot). Look for the sun in the periphery.

Watch the horizon. Horizon lines should be level, and in general, not placed in the center of the composition.

Watch the sky. "Blah" skies have no place in a great photo. If the sky isn't deep blue, contrasted by white clouds, or intensely colorful, compose your shot without it.

Watch the image area. Look for wasted space, light/dark areas, and distracting elements. Before you press the shutter button (or cable release), make your eyes follow around the rectangle of the viewing screen.

2

The Blue Ridge Mountains

Come with us on an adventure through the Blue Ridge Mountains. Our fascination with the natural phenomenon of falling water has brought us here in search of waterfalls. In our endeavor, we have discovered a region rich in natural and human history and encountered physical beauty so compelling that it defies description. It is said that to share a joy is to multiply it. We would like to share the joy of our discoveries with you.

The Blue Ridge Mountains run from southeastern Pennsylvania to northwestern Georgia. They form the eastern portion of the Appalachian Mountains, the great mountain system that extends sixteen hundred miles from Quebec Province to Alabama. In Virginia, the Blue Ridge Mountains divide the Piedmont from the Shenandoah Valley. In North Carolina, they form the eastern section of a mountain chain that is more than seventy-five miles wide and includes the Black Mountains and the Great Smokies.

When seen from a distance, the forested slopes of the Blue Ridge project their bluish tone because water droplets and gas molecules are released into the air by the trees. William Byrd of Virginia was one of the first to note this ever-present blue color in 1728 when he surveyed the boundary between Virginia and North Carolina. Byrd described the distant horizon as "ranges of blue clouds rising one above another." Sadly, however, research is showing that these views are changing at an alarming rate due to the rapidly increasing haze of man-made pollution.

The story of the formation of the Blue Ridge Mountains is not a simple one. These mountains are believed to be among the oldest in the world. Knowing something of their complicated history helps explain why the mountains exist in their present form, supporting the life that exists here.

One current concept of the geologic change is the "plate tectonics" theory: the earth's crust is made up of gigantic, rigid plates of rock that are floating on the hot liquid mantle below. These crusts are always moving—grinding against one another, fusing together and then breaking apart again.

The process that formed the Appalachians and the Blue Ridge began more than a billion years ago. Miles beneath the surface of the earth, molten magma slowly solidified into the core of what we now know as the Blue Ridge Mountains. Over millions of years, this "basement rock" was folded and uplifted, collided with other land masses, lay under giant shallow seas, eroded, and was once again thrust upward.

The last significant event probably occurred two hundred million years ago when eastern North America collided with a continental fragment that was to become Africa. This collision caused the sea floor to fold, lift, and break apart. The older underlying layer of rock tilted upward and slid over the younger layer, creating the Appalachians. The continents fused for a period of perhaps fifty million years and then split again, the Atlantic Ocean filling the void between the separating land masses.

So, the mountains were formed, but there is more to the story. The rolling mountains we see today were once as jagged and craggy as the Himalayas. The rounded peaks of the Blue Ridge are largely a product of mechanical and chemical erosion. These forces have sculpted the mountains into peaceful swells shrouded with blue mist. Wind, water and gravity continue to etch the face of the landscape inch by inch.

The history of the people who have lived in these mountains for centuries is as interesting as the history of the mountains' formation. Archaeological research has shown traces of human habitation in this area as early as 8,000 B.C. Evidence found at various sites throughout

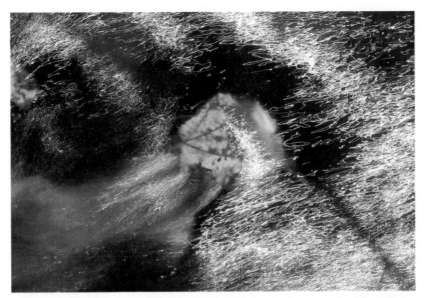

Water running over rocks was a major force in shaping the Blue Ridge Mountains we know today. Photo by Frank Logue.

the mountains indicates that people have been in the Blue Ridge continuously since that time. Indian tribes lived peacefully off this land before the coming of the white man. The first white men were hunters and traders in search of pelts. Many pioneers were kept away by tales of savages and other horrors; at the same time, the native Indians were being exterminated by other Indian raiders, the white man's "whiskey," and smallpox brought by fur traders and pioneers.

The colonists who came here were hardy stock. They were Scotch-Irish immigrants who had survived hard times in northern Ireland, and Germans who came to escape the horrible conditions of the Thirty Years' War. The Scotch-Irish and Germans were joined by Englishmen from the coastal regions.

Before the American Revolution, many rebellious colonists entrenched themselves in the mountains. From their mountain strongholds, they fought and defeated the King's men during the Revolution. Later, the Cherokee would be the foe. Eventually, the area became entirely the white man's domain.

Because of their physical isolation, these Appalachian pioneers became self-sufficient. Schooling was rare. While many of the original settlers could read and write, these skills gradually slipped away. Religion was the major influence on the lives of these people. Traveling ministers carried the gospel to the isolated areas and were often the only outsiders. An old mountain saying, "Thar's nothing about in this weather but crows and Methodist ministers," hints at the ever-present influence of religion on a people shut off from outside civilization.

Roads were barely passable, when they existed at all. Miners and loggers, enticed by rich ore veins and lush forests, depleted resources and departed. The mountain folk were left as destitute as before and their land was desecrated.

The coming of the automobile, coupled with the increase in road building, brought change to the highlands. Electricity and modern conveniences made life somewhat easier for the mountaineers but they maintained their self-sufficiency and their mountain customs.

With the Blue Ridge Parkway came an interest in the lives of these colorful people who occupy the mountains and valleys of the Blue Ridge. Part of the stated purpose of the Blue Ridge Parkway is to preserve the history and culture of the highlanders who call this home.

Just as we are intrigued by the history of the mountains and their inhabitants, we are captivated by the diversity of natural wonders. There is no more ecologically complex woodland area in North America. Thousands of species have developed here over millions of years of evolution.

The dramatic upheavals and shifting that formed the mountains also contributed to the great variety of plant life. Forerunners of rare botanical specimens were deposited in coves created by ancient glaciers.

The abundant rainfall, the mild climate and the great variance in elevation make the Blue Ridge a paradise for botanists. Driving from the foothills of the Blue Ridge to the higher elevations, you encounter the same plant life zones that you would find driving from Georgia to Canada. Trees vary from the sycamore and river birch typical of southeastern stream bottoms, to spruce and fir forests similar to those found in northern Maine.

The naturalist will also find the animal life of the region diverse and plentiful. Ground hogs, known as "whistle pigs," are frequently seen. There are also beaver, deer, bear, elk, fox, opossum, chipmunk, squirrel, and skunk. Bird watchers in the Blue Ridge have a great opportunity because a major migratory flyway follows the mountains.

The Blue Ridge Mountains offer incredible seasonal variety. Spring and summer engage us with their constant palette of colors from brilliant to pastel, showcased against a tapestry of greens. Wildflowers, laurel, rhododendron, and flame azalea provide a procession of color that gives way to the spectacular blaze of fall. The muted tones of winter often belie the unpredictability of this season. The rime that adorns trees and rocks warns us of the chill but provides a magnificent, sparkling picture. The clear, unobstructed panoramas in winter are beyond compare.

The Blue Ridge Parkway forms the backbone of this marvelous scenic region. From Shenandoah National Park in Virginia to the Great Smoky Mountains National Park in North Carolina, it provides a platform from which to survey all the wonders of the entire area. Writing in 1969 in *The Blue Ridge Parkway*, Harley E. Jolley describes it as "a road of unlimited horizons, a grand balcony."

The Parkway is also a masterful feat of engineering that has preserved the physical integrity and the cultural heritage of the Southern Highlands. But few of the millions of tourists who travel the Blue Ridge Parkway each year have any concept of the hard labor, the politics and the dreams that were involved in making the Parkway a reality. Considering the countless hardships and adversities, it is astonishing that the United States' first rural national parkway was ever completed.

The Blue Ridge Parkway was designed as a depression-era project to provide desperately needed jobs for the poverty-stricken people of the southern highlands. The National Park Service archives does not recognize a single originator of the idea. However, several people have taken credit, including Theodore E. Straus of Maryland, a member of the Public Works Administration at the time of the Parkway's inception.

As early as 1909, Colonel Joseph Hyde Pratt, head of the North Carolina Geological Survey, dreamed of a scenic highway through the Blue Ridge Mountains. He even had a short section built before World War I diverted funds and manpower away from the project.

Several historians give credit for the Parkway to Virginia's Senator Harry F. Byrd. Byrd was with President Franklin D. Roosevelt on an August day in 1933 when Roosevelt was on an inspection tour of the Civilian Conservation Corp in the Shenandoah National Park. Roosevelt was very impressed with the Shenandoah's Skyline Drive, and Byrd suggested the grandiose scheme of constructing a road connecting the Shenandoah National Park and the Great Smoky Mountains National Park. Roosevelt was enthusiastic and the wheels were set in motion. Secretary of the Interior, Harold L. Ickes, was asked to determine the route.

The problems of the Parkway were just beginning and would not be resolved until 1968. The project faced incredible obstacles, including debate over the actual path the road would take. Original plans directed the Parkway through North Carolina, Tennessee and Virginia. Bitter fights between politicians from Tennessee and North Carolina created a difficult position for Secretary Ickes. Amidst great protest from Tennessee officials, he opted for the so-called North Carolina route, stating that he found it to be more scenic.

There were many problems obtaining right-of-way, especially through the Cherokee Indian Reservation, which is the final link to the Great Smoky Mountains National Park. After years of haggling between Cherokee and government officials, the Parkway was routed along the ridges to the northwest of the Reservation, just north of the town of Cherokee.

The first rocks of the Parkway were blasted near Cumberland Knob Area (North Carolina) on September 11, 1935, but it was fifty-two years before the last six-and-one-half miles across Grandfather Mountain were completed. The owners were intensely opposed to the route and final right-of-way was not granted until October 22, 1968. This missing link included the Linn Cove Viaduct, said to be one of the most intricate, segmented, concrete bridges ever constructed. One of twelve bridges in the system, this engineering marvel carries vehicles 1,240 feet across the face of Grandfather Mountain. The final section of the Blue Ridge Parkway was completed and dedicated on September 11, 1987.

In July of 1934, Secretary Ickes notified the National Park Service that he wanted the agency to maintain and administer the Parkway. The Congressional Bill to this effect was hotly debated and barely passed the vote. It was signed into law by President Roosevelt on June 22, 1936.

The Parkway begins at milepost 0 at Rockfish Gap, the southern entrance to Virginia's Shenandoah National Park. For 469 miles, this scenic roadway closely follows the highest ridges of the Blue Ridge Mountains. It ends at milepost 469.1, the entrance to the Great Smoky Mountains National Park and the land of the Cherokee. Along the way, the Parkway reaches altitudes of over 6,000 feet, with an average elevation of 3,500 feet. For the first 355 miles, the Parkway closely follows the Blue Ridge in a southwesterly direction. For the remaining 111 miles, it follows the southern end of the imposing Black Mountains and threads through the Craggies, the Pisgahs, and the Balsams.

Traveling the Parkway, the visitor is treated to a multitude of panoramic views varying from dense forests to mile-high mountains. There are plateaus and farmland valleys where early settlers lived. There are meadows lush with wildflowers and old farm buildings and home-steads. The cultural sites and the sheer physical beauty make for a journey rich in both history and inspiring scenery.

The one thing that you will not see on your journey is commercial development. As a parkway, this road is designed and administered as any other national park, complete with exhibits, displays, and interpretive signs. Park rangers work closely with naturalists, agronomists, and environmentalists to protect and restore what lies within the Parkway's domain.

Geographically located within one day's drive of one-half of the nation's population, the Blue Ridge Parkway is not meant to be "a road to somewhere." It is a destination in itself. Millions of visitors come here for the camping facilities, trout-laden streams, bike paths, picnic grounds, horseback-riding, cross-country skiing, and of course, the hiking trails.

The crown jewel of the Blue Ridge Parkway is at its northern end, where Shenandoah National Park straddles an eighty-mile stretch of the Blue Ridge Mountains. The Park varies in width from one to thirteen miles and covers almost two hundred thousand acres, 95% of which is forest. The Shenandoah River lies to the west and Piedmont country to the east.

Shenandoah is an Indian name. Some say it means "daughter of the stars." Another interpretation is "river of high mountains." Either name is an apt description of the long, narrow park on the crest of the mountains. The 105-mile Skyline Drive winds through the Park atop the mountains. To take a trip through Shenandoah along the Skyline Drive is said to be like "riding across the top of Virginia."

The Shenandoah National Park was established in response to a need for a national park to serve the heavily-populated East Coast. However, it has served another purpose, even more important by today's standards. The Park, with its predominantly deciduous forest ecosystem, is a fine example of nature's ability to restore itself. This mountain land had been terribly abused by hunters and ranchers, miners and loggers. After the Park was established in the 1930s and the park service applied principles of conservation, the land regenerated and the vegetation and animal life most suited to its particular habitat was re-established. For this reason, Shenandoah is designated a "recycled park."

Two federal projects were instrumental in the development of the Shenandoah National Park, even before it was officially established. One was the Skyline Drive, which was planned to generate jobs in the economically depressed area. President Herbert Hoover authorized the use of drought relief funds for the construction, which began in 1931. The second was the Civilian Conservation Corp, which contributed a great deal to Shenandoah. The CCC was created in 1933 to provide jobs, as well as speed preparation for the Park. Several camps were established in the area and the men were given responsibility for fire-fighting, erosion control, and landscaping. Many of the Park's beautiful trails and facilities were built by the CCC.

In addition to providing a scenic route in Virginia, the Skyline Drive made another significant contribution. While many dreamed of a roadway along the crest of the Blue Ridge Mountains, it was not until President Franklin D. Roosevelt toured a completed portion of the Skyline Drive in 1933, that the Blue Ridge Parkway was on its way to reality.

Shenandoah was approved by Congress in 1926 as a site for a southern national park, the first in the East. However, while federal funds had been used to build the Skyline Drive and fund CCC projects in the area, no federal monies were appropriated for building the Park. Western parks had been established on federal land. Never before had populated private land been designated for a park. There was no precedent for such a purchase, which had to be made with donated funds.

The campaign to create and fund the park involved the untiring efforts of thousands of private citizens, as well as many employees of the state of Virginia. Senator Harry F. Byrd was an enthusiastic supporter. A total of $1.3 million was pledged by Virginia's citizens, and the State Legislature added another $1 million.

A great deal of partisan lobbying went into the site selection for the Park. George Freeman Pollock, an entrepreneur and owner of the Skyline Resort in northern Virginia, was instrumental in the selection. Pollock was a great showman, and his enthusiasm and energy were tremendous assets in his efforts to have his site chosen. He also loved the Blue Ridge passionately. Pollack once paid a lumberman ten dollars per tree not to cut a grove of one hundred giant hemlocks. You can still see the virgin stand that he saved at Limberlost, an area where the trees are estimated to be three or four hundred years old.

Finally, after years of fights and lawsuits, the state of Virginia had clear title to more than 250 square miles of the Blue Ridge Mountains. Virginia presented this land to the United States on December 12, 1935. The Park was dedicated by President Roosevelt on July 13, 1936. For perhaps the first time in history, the government had obtained land in order to preserve it in its natural state, rather than develop it.

Entrance stations at four different points unofficially split the Park into northern, central, and southern sections. The northern portion of the Park, close to Washington, D.C., receives the most visitors. The central part contains the Park's primary overnight lodging accommodations. The southern section, which has no visitor center and few facilities, offers the most beautiful backcountry. The Park provides 500 miles of hiking trails, and the Skyline Drive runs roughly parallel to about 95 miles of the Appalachian Trail. Many hikers of the Appalachian Trail consider this portion to be one of the most beautiful.

The Park features two visitor centers, four major campgrounds, and seven picnic areas. Visitors to the Park can also stay at the one-hundred-year-old Skyland Lodge founded by George Freeman Pollock.

Often called a "gentle wilderness," Shenandoah National Park offers many varied habitats. Each of these habitats boasts unique features. One of the most unusual areas is the five-square-mile plateau known as Big Meadows, located at an elevation of 3,500 feet. Big Meadows has the greatest variety of plant life in the Park, with at least 800 species. There is also a wide variety of animal life here, the only known place in Shenandoah where you can find a nesting song sparrow or a jumping mouse.

Other areas of the Park offer their own unrivaled features. At Big Devil's Stairs, you can find the oldest trees, which are inaccessible to timbering. Hawksbill, at 4,051 feet, is the highest point in the Park and contains remnant red spruce and forests of balsam fir. Painted trillium can only be found at Laurel Prong. If you climb the ridge trail of popular Old Rag Mountain, you will stand on granite boulders that are part of the basement rock that was formed billions of years ago.

The life in Shenandoah forms a vast and complex natural society that is ever-changing. The forest is an ecosystem with many life forms. The flora include rose azalea, lady slipper orchids, jack-in-the-pulpit, interrupted fern, and over 1,500 other plants. Animal life abounds in the Park as well. Three large animals that disappeared before the Park was formed have been re-established: white-tailed deer, wild turkey, and black bear. There are over 300 species of birds and mammals and about 1,000 species of spiders.

Stop at the Byrd Visitor Center and learn about the Park's geology and history. Or enjoy one of the many hiking trails, a perfect place to reflect on what happens when nature is allowed to take its course without the meddling of humans. This Park has demonstrated very powerfully the ability of the natural world to restore itself. The message of Shenandoah, "river of high mountains," is one of hope for the future of our planet.

If Shenandoah is the crowning glory of the Blue Ridge Parkway, the Great Smoky Mountains National Park is the pot of gold at the end of the rainbow. Located at the southern end of the Parkway, this Park is a treasure chest filled with hiking trails, beautiful campsites, scenic cycling paths, and rivers for fishing and inner-tubing.

The Great Smoky Mountains are part of the Blue Ridge Mountains and the Cherokee called the area Shaconage, "place of blue smoke." The bluish mist that pervades the valleys and hovers over the Blue Ridge Mountains is even more visible in the Smokies, creating a mysterious and eerie hue.

The Cherokee Indians were the first inhabitants of the Great Smoky Mountains. While geologists have their theories about how the mountains were formed, the Cherokee have their own version. Legend has it that a great buzzard was sent down from the sky to find a dry place for everyone to live. Over Cherokee land, the buzzard became very weary and dropped close to the earth. His beating wings struck the soft earth, forming the mountains and valleys and creating the Indians' homeland.

What nature, or legendary buzzards, so miraculously created, man has endangered. Heavy logging stripped the Smokies of vegetation and choked the streams with silt. Brook trout and many other native animals were dying as a result.

A St. Louis librarian named Horace Kephart was one of the first to recognize the value of the Great Smoky Mountains. He came to the Great Smokies in 1904 to recover from ill-health and grew to love the mountains and woodlands. Appalled by the wide-scale decimation of the land, Kephart worked doggedly for years to have the Smokies preserved as a national park. In *Our Southern Highlands*, he wrote of his years in Deep Creek, Hazel Creek, and Bryson City. This sensitive writing helped alert the public to the fact that the mountains were being destroyed.

In 1923, Mr. and Mrs. Willis P. Davis and Colonel David Chapman of Knoxville, Tennessee, formed the Great Smoky Mountains Conservation Association. Under the leadership of Colonel Chapman, and with the influence of others such as Horace Kephart, groups in North Carolina and Tennessee began to raise money to buy the land. Philanthropist John D. Rockefeller contributed $5 million to the cause. With the help of all these contributors, the Great Smoky Mountains National Park was established on June 15, 1934.

Like Shenandoah, the Great Smoky Mountains National Park

incorporated private land, which had to be purchased from individuals. Once again, there were many questions concerning titles and rights-of-way. Finally, the Park was officially dedicated by Roosevelt on September 2, 1940.

The Park sits astride the border of North Carolina and Tennessee. Elevations range from 840 feet at the mouth of Abrams Creek to 6,642 feet at Clingmans Dome. There are 850 miles of trails and footpaths, including 70 miles of the Appalachian Trail. These pathways thread through the Park, leading to coves, balds, rushing streams, and waterfalls.

In earlier times, the Smokies stood as a giant barrier between middle America and the East. Today they are accessible to all and offer a wide variety of outdoor attractions. From the Blue Ridge Parkway on the North Carolina side of the Park, the first stop is the Oconaluftee Visitor's Center, which is open year-round. Here, you can get Park information and literature about the Smokies. Adjacent to the visitors center is the Pioneer Farmstead, an exhibit that shows how the early mountain people lived.

Just north of the visitor center on Newfound Gap Road, Mingus Mill, a large, water-powered grist mill, grinds corn daily from mid April through October.

"Always clear and fragrant..." wrote Horace Kephart about the forests of the Smokies, and so they are. The Park is a wildlands sanctuary, preserving some of the world's finest examples of temperate deciduous forest. Over 130 species of trees exist, broadleaf trees dominate in the coves and conifer forests cover the crests at the highest elevations. This is the largest remaining virgin forest of the eastern American wilderness, covering an estimated one hundred thousand acres, or 20% of the Park. Of the old growth forest that remains in the eastern United States, 90% lies within the Great Smoky Mountains National Park.

The Park itself takes in nearly 800 square miles. Within its boundaries, there are a wealth of natural wonders. The annual rainfall in the Park is over 85 inches per year at the higher elevations, equivalent to that of a rainforest. This abundant rainfall and the fertile soil have encouraged the development of a world-renowned variety of flora, with more than fifteen thousand kinds of flowering plants. Many plants in the higher elevations are more typical of New England and Canada than of the southeastern United States.

An additional attraction is the diversity of animal life. There are more than 400 species of animals and 200 species of birds. Twenty-seven species of salamanders make this area the country's salamander capital. There are at least 52 species of fur-bearing animals, including bear, deer, and wild boar. The wild boar are not a native species and pose a threat to the ecosystem because they are destroying wildflowers and the nests and eggs of ground-nesting birds. Park officials are working to remove these animals.

The United Nations has designated the Great Smoky Mountains National Park as an International Biosphere Reserve because of its abundance and variety of plant and animal life. The Park is managed by the National Park Service as a natural and wild environment.

Of all the many treasures to be found in these two Parks and along the Parkway, the most precious are the water resources. The Blue Ridge is laced with many miles of rivers and streams. In essence, the mountains exist because of water. They were molded by the force of water, and water continues to sculpt the valleys and ridges. The nature and personality of the Blue Ridge Mountains are intrinsically tied to the mystery and magic of the waters.

We came to see the waterfalls, and we learned about the complex interrelationship between man and nature. The process of millions of years of evolution determined the type of plant and animal life that would survive in this region. The various people who came from far and wide combined to form the hardy Appalachian pioneers who lived off this land.

We came to see the waterfalls, and we found the Blue Ridge Parkway, that undulating ribbon of highway that connects two parks. The road exists as a monument to men who were committed to providing us all with a view from the mountaintops.

We came to see the waterfalls, and we discovered the Shenandoah

National Park and the Great Smoky Mountains National Park. These parks are being preserved because people are waking up to the possibility of losing our valuable resources.

We came to see the waterfalls, and we take away a sense of the mystery and majesty of the mountains. When we answer the water's call, we fall under the spell of these enchanted woodlands.

Come and see the waterfalls of the Blue Ridge. Enjoy the peace that the mountains offer. Take a moment to consider the abundant beauty we have at hand and the long-range wisdom of preserving all of this for future generations.

And, by all means, share the joy....

3

Luray

When the time came to decide on a location for the headquarters of Shenandoah National Park, the Park Service selected Luray. An administrative history report explains that the Park Service chose Luray because the townspeople were the earliest and most enthusiastic supporters of the project. Luray's location also added to its appeal. The town lies on US 211, nine miles west of the entrance to the Park's central section.

When the people living on the mountain had to be resettled, many moved to Luray and nearby communities. In turn, the Park employed people from Luray. The town provided mail service, and farms in the valley supplied staples to those working up on the mountain. The Park offices were first located downtown, then moved in 1940 to the "outskirts," five miles east of Luray on US 211.

In the early 1700s, Lt. Governor Alexander Spotswood and the Knights of the Golden Horseshoe ventured through the area. Pioneers began homesteading in the county by the mid 1700s. Luray, the county seat of Page County, was established in 1812 and incorporated in 1871.

Several sources link the name of the town to the Indian word Lorrain, which loosely translates to "crooked waters." But the information sheet *Facts about Luray, Virginia*, printed by the Page County Chamber of Commerce, tells a different story about the origin of the town's name. The Marie family, who were the first settlers in the area, named the town after their grandparents' home—Luray, France.

The county's elevation rises to over four thousand feet in the mountains of the Blue Ridge and drops to almost six hundred feet at the banks of the South Fork of the Shenandoah River, which flows west of town. This historic river may be experienced from a canoe or an innertube. Shenandoah River Outfitters offers daily trips from April through October. You can choose an all-day paddle on beginning whitewater or a half-day float on flatwater. One price includes almost everything you need—equipment, shuttle, even a map. Meals, music, and overnighters can be arranged upon request.

While the county supports poultry and cattle farms and a few small businesses, Luray flourishes as a tourist town, often referred to as the "travel center of the Northern Shenandoah Valley." This title is due in part to Luray Caverns, the largest cave in the East and the most popular, with a half million visitors each year. Luray Caverns also carries the distinction of being a Registered Natural Landmark.

This underground world lies beneath the Shenandoah Valley. It was discovered in August, 1878, by Andrew Campbell and Benton Stebbins, using only a rope and a candlestick. Luray Caverns, a series of rooms linked together by passageways, contains stalactites and stalagmites, cascades and crystal pools, immense columns, and interesting formations. Saturated with color, this example of nature's handiwork rivals much of the scenery above ground.

Open every day of the year, Luray Caverns offers one-hour tours, scheduled every twenty minutes. Guides lead you to named features like the Wishing Well, where millions of coins are collected and donated to national health organizations, and the Great Stalacpipe Organ, the world's largest natural musical instrument. The Organ is explained in a brochure for Luray Caverns: "Stalactites, tuned to concert pitch and accuracy, are struck by electronically controlled, rubber-tipped plungers to produce music of symphonic quality." Credit for this brilliant creation goes to inventor Leland W. Sprinkle.

In addition to exploring the caverns, this attraction hosts the "Historic Car and Carriage Caravan" and the "Luray Singing Tower."

The first is a fascinating museum that portrays the history of transportation. The second is a carillon that serenades the locals with forty-seven bells.

The Caravan's car collection totals over one hundred antiques, including a distinguished exhibit of some of the oldest cars in the country—all still running. To name a few: 1892 Benz, 1906 Ford, 1907 Buick, 1908 Baker Electric, 1907 Buick, 1911 Hupmobile, and 1913 Stanley Steamer.

The Tower sings from March through October. Carillonneur David Breneman conducts recitals that last almost an hour. The forty-seven bells of the carillon range in weight from 12.5 pounds to 7,640 pounds (Wow!).

If you plan to stay in Luray, try the Luray Caverns Motels, two motels conveniently located at either entrance to the Caverns. The historic Mimslyn Hotel, "Grand Old Inn of Virginia," awaits with fifty rooms, while Yogi Bear's Jellystone Park offers shaded trailer and tent sites, as well as cabins.

If you only have a little time to spare, head straight for the Skyline Drive. The central section of Shenandoah National Park has two wonderful camping and lodging facilities—Skyland (mileposts 41.7 and 42.5) and Big Meadows (mileposts 51 and 51.2)—which are discussed further in the waterfall entries that follow.

Your first stop should be Thornton Gap, the entrance (from the north) to the central section of the Park. Thornton Gap lies at 2,304 feet and a trail leads up another 1,200 feet to Mary's Rocks for a terrific view east and west of the Skyline Drive. Facilities at Thornton Gap include the Panorama Restaurant, an information office, and a gift shop.

Head south on the Drive to enjoy the central section of Shenandoah. Park literature lists five waterfall hikes in this section. Trails to Lewis Falls, Dark Hollow Falls, and the waterfalls of Whiteoak Canyon provide more than a day's worth of walking. If you want to see the other two falls in the central section, inquire about Rose River Falls and Cedar Run Falls at the Byrd Visitor Center (milepost 51).

Lewis Falls

2.9 mile loop, Strenuous

Lewis Falls Trail, one of the many side trails along the famous Appalachian Trail, combined with a 1-mile stretch of the Appalachian Trail creates a wonderful loop hike to Lewis Falls. The 2,144-mile Appalachian Trail, which runs from Mt. Katahdin in Maine to Springer Mountain in Georgia, has its longest section (536 miles) in the state of Virginia. Ninety-four of those miles are located in the Park.

Lewis Falls Trail (blue blazes) crosses the Appalachian Trail, then descends to the falls. A spur trail (150 feet) brings you to a viewing area near the top of Lewis Falls, a sheer drop of eighty-one feet. The creek originates at the "housed-in" Lewis Spring on the Appalachian Trail, just south of the service road where this loop hike picks up the Appalachian Trail. Lewis Spring eventually flows into Hawksbill Creek.

A rugged section of trail leads to the service road. Turn right and hike a short distance to pick up the Appalachian Trail (white blazes) on the left. The 1-mile stretch of the Appalachian Trail provides a gradual climb to Blackrock, elevation 3,721 feet. The view west from beneath this set of sheer cliffs is extraordinary. The overlook takes in the Shenandoah Valley and the Massanutten Mountain Range, as well as the distant Alleghenies.

Big Meadows, the location of the trailhead, sits one mile off the Skyline Drive. This resort and recreation facility offers a lodge, dining room, gift shop, amphitheater, picnic grounds, and the largest campground in the Park. President Roosevelt dedicated Shenandoah National Park at the Meadows on July 3, 1936.

Big Meadows gets its name from the beautiful grassy opening, the only treeless area in the Park. At least a portion of this meadow has been cleared since ancient times. The Indians may have found the natural clearing, the result of a lightning-induced fire, or they may have cleared it. Whatever the case, they took advantage of the opening as a hunting and camping area. Early settlers expanded the clearing for cattle grazing. By the early 1900s, Big Meadows was a combination of meadows, pastures, and garden plots. Since the Park's opening, small sections have been kept clear, but the rest is reverting to forest.

Directions: From Luray, head east on US 211 for 5 miles to the headquarters office of the Shenandoah National Park. After stopping to ask questions and gather brochures and maps, continue east on US 211 for another 4 miles to Thornton Gap Entrance Station (milepost 31.5). Get on the Skyline Drive heading south and go to milepost 51.2. Turn right onto the entrance road for Big Meadows and travel 1 mile. Park in the lot for the picnic area and locate the trail behind the amphitheater.

Dark Hollow Falls

1.6 miles roundtrip, Moderate

The shortest trail in the Park that leads to a waterfall follows Hogcamp Branch to Dark Hollow Falls. The length of this waterfall trail and the location of the trailhead, across from the Byrd Visitor Center, make Dark Hollow Falls Trail the most popular trail in the Park.

Before beginning this hike, stop in at the Byrd Visitor Center, which houses interpretive displays about the people who lived in these mountains. The center is named after Harry F. Byrd, Sr., a prominent Virginia governor and U.S. senator who hiked all the Park's peaks. He climbed his favorite, Old Rag Mountain, every year.

North across the Drive from the visitor center, you'll find the trailhead for Dark Hollow Falls, at an elevation of 3,490 feet. The blue-blazed trail descends steeply along the branch to an excellent viewpoint at the base of the falls. The narrow cascade courses seventy feet over a series of terraced drops. Hogcamp Branch flows into the Rose River.

The near-vertical falls flow over greenstone, a reminder of one period of volcanic activity that occurred hundreds of millions of years ago. The dykes of greenstone remain where lava erupted from long fissures in the granite rock. This erosion-resistant rock tops much of the crest of the Blue Ridge and can be seen at several places in the Park, including Stony Man and Hawksbill Mountain.

In addition to the waterfall, you can visit Cave Cemetery. Go beyond Dark Hollow Falls, intersect the Rose River Fire Road (where you'll find a trail marker with mileage), and hike left a short distance. People in the mountains have buried their loved ones here since the 1800s. The park service opens the fire road to locals so they can continue to use the cemetery.

Directions: From Luray, travel to the Skyline Drive (see directions under Lewis Falls) and go south to milepost 50.5. Dark Hollow Parking Area is on the left, just north of Big Meadows. The trailhead is at the north end of the parking area.

Waterfalls in Whiteoak Canyon
7.2 miles roundtrip, Strenuous

Cutting a deep canyon on its way down the mountainside to Old Rag Valley, Whiteoak Run boasts a 1.3-mile stretch with six waterfalls. Numbers denote each waterfall instead of names. Dropping eighty-six feet, Whiteoak Falls #1 is the second highest in the Park, shorter than Big Falls in the northern section by five feet.

Park literature lists the heights of the other falls as follows: #2, sixty-two feet; #3, thirty-five feet; #4, forty-one feet; #5, forty-nine feet; and #6, sixty feet. The heights of the falls add up to 333 feet, but from the trailhead at 3,516 feet, the blue-blazed Whiteoak Canyon Trail drops 2,000 feet before reaching Whiteoak Falls #6.

The trailhead is located near the Drive in a resort and recreation facility called Skyland. George Freeman Pollock, a colorful man and a born naturalist who helped establish the Park, came to the area from Washington, D.C., in the 1890s. His private mountain retreat began as a tent camp, then he built log cottages.

Today, Skyland is one of the main concession operations in the Park. The north entrance to Skyland sits at 3,680 feet, the highest point of the Skyline Drive. You can stay at the Massanutten Lodge or rent a rustic cabin. Facilities include a conference hall and a restaurant that offers mountain cuisine and live entertainment. The Skyland stables provides daily rides on a network of horse trails.

Within the first mile of the trail, you will cross a branch of Whiteoak Run, the Old Rag Fire Road, and the Limberlost Trail. Limberlost, an area along the Skyline Drive covered in huge hemlocks, was named by Pollock because the stand of big trees reminded him of something from "Girl of the Limberlost" by General Stratton Porter. As the largest grove of virgin hemlock in the Park, these grand trees still stand because Pollock loved the area so much that he paid off the loggers who were planning to cut the hemlocks.

After Limberlost, the trail becomes steeper, converging with and then crossing Whiteoak Run. Pollock used to bring guests here for his famous BBQ in the old Skyland days. Just beyond the junction with the Skyland-Meadows Horse Trail, a primitive overlook affords a good view of the first waterfall (at 2.3 miles).

As you switchback down the steep canyon, occasional views of the other falls open up. You must look carefully to catch every waterfall. After crossing a side creek (Negro Run), the trail cuts in close to the creek just below Whiteoak Falls #6.

The name of the canyon, the run, and the waterfalls came from the once-predominant whiteoak. Today, hemlock rules the forest in Whiteoak Canyon. Ash and tulip also provide shade. Because of overuse and the sensitive nature of the area, camping is prohibited between Whiteoak Falls #1 and the junction with Cedar Run Link Trail, beyond Whiteoak Falls #6.

Directions: From Luray, travel to the Skyline Drive (see directions under Lewis Falls) and go south to milepost 42.6. Whiteoak Canyon Parking Area is on the right, across from the south entrance to Skyland. The trailhead is at the upper end of the parking area.

4

Waynesboro

Waynesboro is located in the center of the eastern portion of the Shenandoah Valley. Nearby at Afton Mountain, the Blue Ridge Parkway meets the Shenandoah National Park's Skyline Drive. The Allegheny Mountains lie to the west, the crests of the Blue Ridge flank the eastern part of the valley.

This part of Virginia is referred to as the state's "crowning glory." And for good reason. From the grandness of the mountaintops to the richness of the valley below, the area offers breathtaking vistas, plenty of outdoor recreation, and many historical and cultural attractions.

The first white man to view the area was a German explorer named John Lederer. In 1669, he gazed upon the Shenandoah Valley from atop the Blue Ridge Mountains and reported his findings of rich, fertile land to the Governor in Williamsburg. Soon frontier farms and villages were established by Scotch, German, Irish, and English.

Waynesboro was originally part of a 1736 land grant from King George II of England to Governor Gooch. Gooch transferred the land to William Beverly. In 1739, Beverly granted 465 acres to Joseph Tees, the proprietor of Tees Tavern, and the village of Teesville was formed on the west bank of the South River. After the Revolutionary War, the town's name was changed to Waynesborough (later shortened to Waynesboro) in honor of the flamboyant General "Mad" Anthony Wayne. Wayne was famous for his reckless courage in combat.

More than half a century later, Basic City was founded on the east side of South River. Waynesboro and Basic City consolidated in 1924 and industrial growth brought an increase in population. By February of 1948, Waynesboro became the twenty-fifth city in Virginia's history to be designated a city "of the first class" under the terms of the state constitution.

Waynesboro is centrally located to many historic landmarks. Thomas Jefferson's Monticello and James Monroe's Ashlawn are both within a thirty minute drive of town. The Woodrow Wilson birthplace, an 1846 Greek Revival townhouse in Waynesboro, is listed as a National Historic Landmark. Some of the original furnishings are still in place, including the crib in which Wilson slept as a baby and the family Bible where the former President's birth is recorded.

The Waynesboro area is home to several famous institutions of learning. Among them are Washington and Lee, Virginia Military Institute, and the University of Virginia, which was founded by Thomas Jefferson, James Madison, James Monroe, and John Marshall. Founded in 1877, the Fisburne Military School is a State and National Historic Landmark. Fisburne occupies the largest privately-owned tract of land adjacent to downtown Waynesboro.

The Museum of American Frontier Culture offers a unique glimpse into the past of this colorful region. Located in nearby Staunton, this living museum presents working farms that illustrate the European influence on America's 18th and 19th century culture. Interpreters in costume demonstrate the German, Northern Irish, and English impact on life in colonial America. The museum conducts programs daily, except on Thanksgiving, Christmas, and New Year's Day.

For the art enthusiast, Waynesboro serves up a full plate. The Shenandoah Valley Art Center is a non-profit organization that is staffed by volunteers and dedicated to promoting the arts in the Shenandoah Valley. In addition to being a showcase for outstanding artists from the region, the center also features exhibits, performances, workshops, and classes in the various creative arts. The center is located at 600 West Main Street and admission is free.

The works of P. Buckley Moss are housed in a museum at 2150

Rossner Avenue. Moss's work is probably among the most recognized anywhere in the country. This internationally known artist is famous for her inimitable style, symbolism, and unique portrayal of the simple lifestyles of the Amish and Mennonite people. The P. Buckley Moss Museum is in a building that resembles the style of houses built in the early 1800s by settlers of this area.

Another fascinating place to visit is Swannanoa, atop nearby Mt. Afton. The Italian Renaissance-style palace, constructed of marble, serves as headquarters for the University of Science and Philosophy founded by Walter and Lao Russell. The Russells were philosophers, artists, and scientists, and the marble palace houses many of their works of art. The terraced sculpture gardens afford incredible views.

One of the most outstanding art events in Waynesboro is the Fall Foliage Festival Art Show. Held in downtown Waynesboro on two weekends each October, the Fall Festival draws more than two hundred artists and craftsmen from all over who display their pottery, metalwork, paintings, photographs, sculpture, and jewelry. The show is reputed to be one of the best such happenings on the East Coast, and the grandeur of the fall foliage surrounding Shenandoah Valley can't be beat.

If you have a penchant for spending or saving money (depending on how you look at it), don't miss the Waynesboro outlet village, cited by *Woman's Day* as one of the southeast's top discount outlets. Architectur-ally-styled like an 18th century Virginia town, the village has a little of everything.

Downtown Waynesboro also offers great shopping opportunities. Our favorite shop, Virginia Metalcrafters, produces some of colonial America's finest brass and iron pieces. An observation booth at the factory allows visitors to watch the artisans using the original technique of pouring molten brass into hand-formed sand molds. Many of the accessories found in Colonial Williamsburg are authentically repro-duced here.

While wonderful and fascinating, the "man-made" attractions of Waynesboro pale in comparison to those nature has to offer. From the Blue Ridge Parkway, you can access George Washington National Forest and the Appalachian Trail. From the Skyline Drive, you can experience

Shenandoah National Park, which provides overlooks, picnic areas, campgrounds, and hiking trails.

The National Park Service operates the Sherando Lake Recreation Area. Located in the mountains about fourteen miles south of Waynesboro, the recreation area offers three family camping loops and a group campground. (You can camp here for fourteen days.) The majority of the facilities are located between two lakes, the largest of which (twenty-four acres) was built by the Civilian Conservation Corps in the 1930s. The upper lake, used primarily for fishing, consists of seven acres. Sherando Lake Recreation Area is a great spot for a picnic and a good base for a variety of day hikes.

Just east of Waynesboro at Rockfish Gap, the southern entrance to the Skyline Drive (milepost 105.4) meets the northernmost point of the Blue Ridge Parkway (milepost 0). Rockfish Gap Tourist Information Center staffs helpful volunteers who will assist you and answer your questions about the Shenandoah Valley, the Skyline Drive, the Parkway, and other area attractions, making it an ideal place to get your bearings and plan your stay. All of the directions to the waterfalls described under Waynesboro start from Rockfish Gap.

Crabtree Falls

3.0 miles roundtrip, Moderate

Crabtree Falls is the highest waterfall east of the Mississippi, depending on how you qualify a waterfall, but there is no doubt that Crabtree Fall is the highest waterfall in Virginia. Crabtree Falls is really a name given to five major waterfalls (and several smaller ones) on Crabtree Creek, which flows into the Tye River. Within a half-mile, the creek drops twelve hundred feet. There is one vertical drop of five hundred feet.

Crabtree Falls is a popular attraction. If you spread out the estimated twenty thousand visitors over a year, you'd have about fifty-five a day. Unfortunately, most people come between May and October. Try squeezing that number into twenty parking spaces. (In March, yours may be the only car in the lot.)

Crabtree Falls is famous for its connection to the well-known television show *The Waltons*. The falls were not shown on television, but the name was referred to several times during the life of the program. The mention of Crabtree Falls was usually in reference to a Sunday outing.

The name "Crabtree" is thought to have come from William Crabtree, who settled in the area in 1777. Some even say he discovered the waterfall. Another noted pioneer, Allen Tye, who did extensive exploration in the Blue Ridge Mountains, is identified as having discovered the Tye River.

The land at the base of the falls was almost developed as a resort area in the late 1960s. Land owner Hugh D. Bolton put up "No Trespassing" signs and stated that he wanted to create something called "Living Waters." The residents of Nelson County encouraged involvement from the forest service, who had purchased acreage around the falls since the 1930s through small acquisitions and land exchanges, acquiring the falls in 1968. By 1972, after many unsuccessful offers to obtain the land at the base of the falls, proceedings began to condemn the two tracts.

The land became part of the George Washington National Forest, and Southern District Representative Jay Robinson secured money from Congress to be used to improve the area around the falls. The waterfall trail has been developed into a showpiece of the Pedlar District. There are wooden stairs, gravel paths, railed overlooks, and a spectacular bridge over the Tye River.

The 110-foot wooden bridge across the Tye River has a most interesting story. It was the first of the trail improvements made by the forest service in the late 1970s. When I read the cost, I thought it must be a misprint—$62,000! Why so much? This beautiful bridge, a laminated arch, was shipped from New York in one piece. Cranes lifted and placed it over the Tye River in 1978.

The trail parallels the Tye River a short distance before crossing on the bridge. Then, the blue-blazed trail follows Crabtree Creek for three miles through a sliver of old hemlock, as well as yellow birch, striped maple, and American elm, to Crabtree Meadows. Or, you can turn around at the last waterfall overlook (1.5 miles) for a hike that also totals three miles. The first of many observation decks begins only seven hundred yards past the Tye River.

Crabtree Falls in the Pedlar District of George Washington National Forest is the highest waterfall in Virginia. It is a series of five major falls and many minor ones that drop more than 1200 feet in a half mile. U.S. Forest Service photo.

Crabtree Meadows is an open area with crab apples and apple trees. In the 1930s, several families lived on the site of Crabtree Meadow Campground, a national forest primitive campsite with water and pit toilets. The Appalachian Trail can be accessed from here via a 0.5-mile side trail.

Crabtree Falls has a fascinating history and offers many nice features, but something I found struck me as most unusual—a pay phone. There is a telephone right after you cross the Tye River—a strange thing to see in the woods. It was put in because of the growing number of accidents at the falls: rescue numbers are posted inside. There have been twenty-one deaths and many injuries at Crabtree Falls. The forest service even maintains a four-wheel-drive road at the top of the falls primarily for use in rescues.

Directions: From Waynesboro, access the Blue Ridge Parkway at milepost 0 and head south to milepost 27.2. Exit onto VA 56 going east (left) and follow the signs to Crabtree Falls (about 6.3 miles). There is a paved parking area on the right and the trail begins at the upper end. To reach Crabtree Meadows, head back towards the Parkway for 2.8 miles and turn left onto SR 826. The upper trailhead is 4 miles down and on the left.

St. Mary's Waterfall

4.4 miles roundtrip, Easy

St. Mary's Waterfall is in St. Mary's Wilderness Area, part of George Washington National Forest. The wilderness tract is over ten thousand acres, making it the largest national forest wilderness area in Virginia. The Virginia Wilderness Bill of 1984 established that all roads in the St. Mary's Wilderness Area must be closed to vehicles and commercial activity. St. Mary's continues to allow only foot traffic within its boundaries.

The elevation varies from 1,700 to 3,600 feet. The highest point is Cellar Mountain, which has rocky bluffs near the base. Surprisingly, the area was never logged. You will find that oak and hickory rule the forest, but you won't find big trees because the soil is not sufficient and the inclines are too rugged. Other vegetation includes sumac, black birch, rhododendron, laurel, and my favorite, blueberries. St. Mary's River and its tributaries contain a large population of native trout and the wild land makes good bear habitat.

The blue-blazed St. Mary's Trail totals 6.2 miles, but the orange-blazed side trail that leads to the waterfall bears off after 1.4 miles. From the barrier gate, hike along the St. Mary's River on an old roadbed and then a dried-up stream. After crossing the river (wading during high water) where the rocks are painted with blue blazes, the St. Mary's Trail bears right and heads toward the crest of the Blue Ridge to Green Pond, a one-acre, high-elevation bog.

Go left instead, through a campsite, and across the St. Mary's River again in order to pick up the 0.8-mile waterfall spur, which leads into the St. Mary's Gorge. The St. Mary's Waterfall spills over a ten-foot ledge between the quartzite walls of this miniature canyon. The large pool at the base is surrounded by jagged boulders and short cliffs.

The touring highlight in the St. Mary's Wilderness is a surface-mining excavation. There is a creek, a trail, and a mountain—all by the name of Mine Bank. For the first fifty years of this century, several mines in the gorge produced manganese and iron ore. A railroad tramway came up the hollow and carried the ore to processing plants.

Evidence of the mining operation remains in the forest. The topographic map printed by the forest service shows four old mine sites located on a section of the St. Mary's Trail beginning less than one mile past the waterfall spur. Several trails in this wilderness area follow the former tramline or old mining roads.

Within the boundaries of the St. Mary's Wilderness Area, there are over fifteen miles of trail, including Mine Bank Trail, Bald Mountain Trail, Cellar Mountain Trail and Cold Springs Trail. Write the Pedlar Ranger District at 2424 Magnolia Avenue, Buena Vista, VA 24416, for a topographic map with trail system information and special considerations.

Directions: From Waynesboro, get on the Blue Ridge Parkway at milepost 0 and head south to milepost 27.2. Exit onto VA 56 going west (right) and travel 3.6 miles to Vesuvius, where SR 608 becomes part of VA 56 for about 0.5 miles. Bear right when SR 608 splits off from VA 56, and drive 2.4 miles to a right turn onto FDR 41. This road becomes gravel within a few hundred yards and ends at a parking area after 1.4 miles. The trailhead is at the upper end beyond the information board.

White Rock Falls

1.8 miles roundtrip, Moderate
White Rock Falls Trail was built in 1979 by the Youth Conservation Corps. The trail is maintained by members of the Tidewater Appalachian Trail Club, who volunteer their time to do upkeep and repair on ten miles of the Appalachian Trail—from Reeds Gap to the Tye River.

The club adopted the White Rock Falls Trail even though it isn't part of the Appalachian Trail. Robert Adkisson, member of the Tidewater Club, has been hiking the trail several times a year for the last four years. He uses a swing blade on the weeds and a chain saw on fallen trees.

Begin at Slacks Overlook (2,800 feet), and after three creek crossings—a footbridge and two rock hops—savor the view of the White Rock Creek Valley from the rocky outcropping. One switchback will take you below the outcropping where there is a small sign tacked to a tree. It says "Falls," indicating the waterfall is straight ahead. (White Rock Falls Trail takes a sharp right and continues 1.6 miles to milepost 18.5, White Rock Gap.) This yellow-blazed trail doesn't stray more than a half mile from the Parkway, yet it is impossible to hear any car noise—just the sounds of the forest.

White Rock Falls is a small-volume falls, but it spills thirty feet into an incredible gorge. The walls of the narrow canyon embrace you on three sides, old-growth hemlocks tower above. Although the creek is small, the pool at the base of the falls is big enough for six to enjoy a swim.

White Rock Creek flows into the North Fork of the Tye River. There is a community called White Rock, a half dozen houses at the place where the two creeks meet. "White rock" refers to the quartz that is so prevalent in the area.

Directions: From Waynesboro, get on the Blue Ridge Parkway at milepost 0 and head south to milepost 19.9, Slacks Overlook (on the right). To find the trailhead, go across the road and walk north for about 60 yards. There is a wooden sign (look down the slope towards the woods) marking the trailhead.

5

Clifton Forge

Clifton Forge has the distinction of being the only town in the entire United States with that name. The saga began, according to geologists, over twelve million years ago. Far beneath the surface, the earth was storing layer upon layer of precious mineral resources for the future. Eons later, after the Jackson River had exposed the rainbow of ore-bearing rock, the story of Clifton Forge began. And that story is as unique as the town's name.

For years, iron was monarch in this section of Virginia, and the economy pivoted on the vast funaces and forges that peppered the hillsides of the Alleghany Mountains. Then, in the early 1900s, iron ore was discovered in the region of the Great Lakes. This midwestern ore was much more accessible than that in the Alleghanies; so by the end of World War I, the iron industry around Clifton Forge was dead. However, the town remained and progressed. The colorful story of Clifton Forge sharply contrasts the grimly abandoned iron furnances that can still be seen dotting the countryside of the Alleghanies.

Clifton Forge is part of an area known as the Alleghany Highlands, which consists of Alleghany County, its county seat of Covington, and Clifton Forge. The area lies west of the Blue Ridge Parkway at the southern tip of the Shenandoah Valley. This part of western Virginia is over eighty-eight percent forested and includes almost 135,000 acres of national forest.

Like much of colonial America, Clifton Forge began as a land grant from King George III to a colonial governor. In this case, the grant was made to Lord Botetourt, Governor of Virginia. In turn, the governor made grants in 1770 and 1772 to a frontiersman named Robert Gallaspy. The tracts were on the north side of the Jackson River and on both sides of what is now Smith Creek.

Of course, the first real inhabitants of what would become Alleghany County were Shawnee, Delaware, and Mingo Indians. Terrified of Indian attack, the pioneers were reluctant to settle in the region. Only the truly adventurous were intrepid enough to locate here, and originally the settlement consisted of only four families living in log cabins.

The history of Clifton Forge reveals some interesting stories about the pioneers and the Indians. One such story concerns a young lady named Katherine Van Stavern. In 1810, Miss Van Stavern's father bought the land that once belonged to Robert Gallaspy. Using the little house where preaching was done on Sundays, Miss Katherine began a school for the few children in the area. It seems our school marm was forever getting herself into scrapes with the Indians. One day, two war-painted "savages" appeared in the schoolhouse door, prepared to scalp the teacher and students. Arriving in the nick of time, Harry Gorhman, the long time friend and admirer of Miss Van Stavern, shot one Indian and sent the other scurrying into the woods.

A few weeks later, Miss Katherine was kidnapped by Indians and taken to their camp. Once again, Harry Gorhman saved the day. He had been hunting near the river and witnessed the kidnapping. Gorhman alerted the settlers, who stole into the Indian camp that night and rescued the damsel in distress. Would you be surprised to learn that the first wedding to take place in the area was that of Miss Katherine Van Stavern to Mr. Harry Gorhman?

The land originally granted to Robert Gallaspy went through several title transfers, eventually coming to Henry Smith of Fifeshire, Scotland, in 1825. Smith was joined by his wife's sister and her husband, Jean and Andrew Williamson, also of Fifeshire. Eventually Henry Smith, who had no children, passed his holdings onto his nephew, David Williamson.

The eastern part of Clifton Forge was originally called Williamson in honor of this large and prominent family.

The village grew up along both sides of the Jackson River. Most of the early settlers were of Scotch-Irish descent and their lifestyle was simple and somewhat severe. Their world existed within the radius of a few miles and centered mostly around the church. The Oakland Grove Presbyterian Church still sits in a little hollow about two miles west of Clifton Forge. Built in 1834 from bricks baked in nearby ovens and carried to the site by saddlebag, the church is the oldest in this part of Virginia. Long known as the "church by the spring," the building still has the original pews of twelve-inch solid chestnut. The church served as a hospital during the War Between the States. Some of the Williamsons are buried in the graveyard.

In the 1800s, the town of Williamson grew and prospered around the iron industry and the railroad. Colonel John Jordan of Lexington operated several iron furnaces and was responsible for the building of a road across North Mountain between Lexington and Clifton Forge. The road, a monumental undertaking, was necessary for wagon access to the furnaces. No one else thought the road could be built, but the colorful Colonel undertook the project and saw it to completion. There is an old abandoned cemetery on the crest of North Mountain that contains the graves of workers who died during the grueling construction of what became known as the Midland Trail.

Colonel Jordan, along with his partner John Irvine, acquired land near the headwaters of the James River, where the Cowpasture and Jackson Rivers meet. The land was rich in soil containing brown hematite ore. It was here, in 1827, that the partners erected the first hot blast furnace in the south. Built on Simpson's Creek, a tributary of the Cowpasture, the furnace was named for the founders' wives, Lucy Jordan and Selina Irvin.

In 1831, the Lucy Selina Furnace and Forge was operated by William Lyle Alexander, an associate in the Jordan iron dynasty. Alexander was from Lexington and named the forge "Clifton" in honor of his father's estate there.

In 1834, after the death of John Irvin, John Jordan's sons Edwin and

Ira took over the operation of the Lucy Selina. A few years later, during the Civil War, the furnace was taken over by the Confederate Government for the production of cannons and cannon balls. The "Merrimac," a famous Confederate ironclad gunboat, was built from iron made in the area. The vessel was blown up by the Confederacy to prevent her from falling into federal hands when the Norfolk Navy Yard was abandoned during the War.

Depressed after the devastation of the war and the loss of his slaves, Edwin Jordan hanged himself, and Harry Firmstone of England took over ownership of the Lucy Selina. He formed the Longdale Company, and in 1873, built the Firmstone Mansion, a twenty-room estate. At the turn of the century, the social season of the area centered around the annual picnic at Firmstone Manor. The mansion now serves as a bed and breakfast.

The Lucy Selina was the first of many such furnaces established here. Alleghany iron ore was known worldwide and was said by blacksmiths to be supreme because it was charcoal iron. The Lucy Selina Forge ceased operation in 1911, but the twin stacks of the furnace still stand east of Clifton Forge on US 60.

Actually, the first iron furnace, or "forge," just may have been built by Robert Gillaspy. The waters of the Jackson River, over millions of years, had worn away the mountain, exposing the colorful layers of mineral-rich shale, quartzite, sandstone, and limestone. The Iron-Gate Gorge (known to tourists today as Rainbow Gap) may have enticed Gillaspy to establish a forge here.

Gillaspy's "forge under the cliffs" could have been the forerunner of the "Old Clifton Forge." An old abandoned cave was found in the Iron-Gate Gorge—a cave that was loaded with iron-ore. The cave also contained the skeletons of two miners and a mule. Their deaths obviously put an end to that endeavor. Then, in 1827, Colonel Jordan obtained the forge. And, well...you know the rest.

The railroad was as important to the development of Clifton Forge as the iron industry. For, without a link to the "western waters" of the Ohio and Mississippi Rivers, the coal and iron of the region could never have helped fuel the Industrial Revolution. The Chesapeake and Ohio

Railway provided Virginia's connection to these western waterways. The C & O, an innovator in steam locomotives, is best known for its long coal trains. However, the railroad also claimed some of the most famous passenger trains in American Railroad history—trains such as the George Washington and the Fast Flying Virginian. And legends about the C & O abound. Who has not heard the famous story of John Henry, the steel driver who beat a steam drill in a race at Big Bend Tunnel in 1872?

In 1882, the Chesapeake and Ohio Railway Company named its new depot Clifton Forge, and the little town became an important junction for the railroad. The railroad became the principal industry of the area and the company purchased much of the property thereabouts. Today, the C & O Historical Archives in Clifton Forge preserves and interprets the history of this railway. Railroad enthusiasts will find a visit here most rewarding.

Along with a rich history, the Alleghany Highlands Area of Virginia has many landmarks to entice the visitor. Follow Colonel John Jordan's original Midland Trail to Humpback Bridge, the only surviving trussed arch in America. This covered bridge, a Virginia Historic Landmark built in 1835, is surrounded by its own state park.

Fort Young near Covington is a reconstruction of a French and Indian War fort that was designed by Geroge Washington. Several other area landmarks on the National Register of Historic Places include the Clifton Forge Post Office (1910) and the Alleghany County Court House in Covington (1911).

Clifton Forge has its share of unique specialty and antique shops such as Roxie's on Main Street. Here you'll find antiques, dollhouses, and miniatures. The Alleghany Highlands Arts and Crafts Center on I-64 is an exhibit, display, and sales center for regional fine arts and hand-crafted products. And the town sports its version of a Fall Foliage Festival, the annual celebration of nature's spectacle of color.

In nearby Hot Springs and Warm Springs are natural rock pools with 98.6-degree Fahrenheit mineral waters famed for their curative properties. At Warm Springs, the baths are housed in their original 18th and 19th century structures and are open mid-April until October. Hot Springs is home to the Homestead, another National Historic Landmark and a five-star resort that has been owned by the same family for over one hundred years.

As you might expect, though, we find nature's bounties to be the most remarkable attributes of the Alleghany Highlands. Among them are the lush George Washington National Forest, the Gathright Wildlife Management Area, which includes 2,530-acre Lake Moomaw, and Douthat State Park.

The North Mountain Trail in the James River District of George Washington National Forest provides some excellent hiking opportunities. This path follows the ridge of North Mountain, and rocky outcroppings along the way are great places to take in the endless panoramas of the James River Valley. The Roaring Rock Recreation Area, south of Clifton Forge, offers hiking to a forty foot waterfall and the ruins of an 1838 iron furnance. And there is year-round fishing in the lakes, river, and streams.

So let's "forge" ahead to some of the liquid miracles of this truly exceptional region.

Stony Run Falls and Blue Suck Falls

8.8 mile loop, Moderate

Stony Run Falls and Blue Suck Falls are located in Douthat State Park, established in the early 1930s as one of the first six state parks in Virginia. The Civilian Conservation Corps left a mark of fine "Depression era" landscaping and wood craftsmanship throughout the Park. Douthat State Park is recognized as a National Registered Historic Landmark.

The Park lies between two ridges and covers close to 4,500 acres. Wilson Creek runs through the Park, north-to-south, and parallels VA 629. A dam, built by the CCC, impounds the fifty-acre Douthat Lake, and a visitor center operates from Memorial Day weekend to Labor Day. The list of facilities is long: store, amphitheater, restaurant, campground, cabins and lodge, boat ramp, and boat rentals. (Whew!) You can lunch under the picnic shelter, swim at designated beaches, fish from the creek or the lake, and of course, go hiking.

Douthat State Park offers more miles of hiking trails than any state park in Virginia. This waterfall loop is part of the forty miles of hiking trails in the Park. The circuit consists of four trails—Stony Run Trail (orange blazes, 4.5 miles); Tuscarora Overlook Trail (yellow blazes, 0.8 miles); Blue Suck Falls Trail (blue blazes, 2.8 miles); and Tobacco House Ridge Trail (yellow blazes, 0.8 miles).

Beginning at the trailhead for Stony Run Trail, you'll climb gradually for 2.5 miles, gaining 300 feet in elevation, to Stony Run Falls. Follow the short side trail to the falls. The ascent continues as you scale Middle Mountain on several switchbacks. Once on Tuscarora Overlook Trail, you'll come to a grassy clearing and a restored CCC cabin. This maintained overlook affords the most beautiful view in the Park looking west down into the basin of Wilson Creek and across towards the distant Beard's Mountain on the Park's east boundary. Blue Suck Trail leads you to another superb view called Lookout Rock (2,560 feet), and then descends on switchbacks through a hollow along Blue Suck Run to cross the base of Blue Suck Falls at 7.5 miles. Don't miss the right onto Tobacco House Ridge Trail, which takes you to Campground C.

The loop trail crosses Stony Run and Blue Suck Run several times— no bridges—so wear weather-proof shoes. Many trails intersect the loop trail; watch the colored blazes carefully.

Both Stony Run Falls and Blue Suck Falls are located on runs by the same names. They originate on Middle Mountain, the highest peak in the Park. Stony Run and Blue Suck Run flow into Wilson Creek below Douthat Lake. The narrow waterfalls both drop about fifty feet, but Blue Suck Falls has three distinct cascades. Try to visit these creeks after a good rain—there are practically no waterfalls if these runs are dry.

Directions: From Clifton Forge, take Exit 8 off I-64 and head north on VA 629 (Douthat Road), which runs through the Park. The office is 7 miles on the right. The parking area for Stony Run Falls is 0.5 miles back down VA 629 on the right. The trailhead is in the center of the parking area. To avoid hiking the additional 0.5 miles along VA 629 at the end of the loop, set a second car (or have someone pick you up) at the bathhouse in Campground C, directly across from the Park's office.

Fallingwater Springs

No hike necessary

"The only remarkable cascade in this country is that of the Falling Spring in Augusta. It is a water of the James River where it is called Jackson's River. It falls over a rock about two hundred feet into the valley below and while not as wide as Niagara it is again half as high." (Thomas Jefferson, "Notes on Virginia," 1778.) A trip to Fallingwater Springs is hard to resist after such an extraordinary endorsement from a famous visitor.

There are two pull-overs. The first is an overlook; the second, a small parking area with a connecting sidewalk back to the overlook. The view is excellent. Fallingwater Creek dives off the bluff–literally leaping as the sign in the parking area describes. From the overlook, you can watch the creek disappear into the valley of Falling Springs.

Falling Springs originates on a 60-acre farm owned by Burton Parker that was once the world's largest watercress farm. The spring is fed from several underground springs–warm and cold–in separate caves. The combination creates a stream temperature that averages 65.6 degrees Fahrenheit.

In the corner of the parking area to the left of the sign, an undeveloped trail (with no railings) awaits the adventurous hiker. Although I would not recommend scrambling down this path, the executive director of the Alleghany Chamber of Commerce said a film crew made it to the bottom with a bulky movie camera and tripod.

Across the road from the waterfall, a bronze plaque affixed to a boulder honors an Indian fighter and courier who saved Fort Lee from the Indians in the late 1700s. The gun powder ran out; the only chance for protecting the fort was a perilous journey to resupply at Camp Union, a three-day roundtrip of 240 miles past enemy forces and through fierce wilderness.

The hero who volunteered when no one else would take on the ride was actually a heroine, a woman named Ann Bailey, often referred to as "Mad Ann." Her famed horse was a black pony called "Liverpool," and the plaque was a project of the local chapter of the Daughters of the American Revolution.

Directions: From Clifton Forge, travel west for 7 miles on US 60 to Exit 16 near Covington. Go north on US 220. (Don't turn right onto VA 687 for the town of Falling Spring.) "Falling Springs Gorge Lookout 1000 feet" is written on a brown sign. Pull into the parking area on the left.

Roaring Run Falls

1.4 mile loop, Moderate

Roaring Run Falls is part of a recreation area in the Jefferson National Forest (elevation 1,200 feet). In the mid 1980s, Roaring Run Trail was designated a National Recreation Trail, which creates a framework of first priority for maintaining scenic quality and doing trail repairs. Because of budget cuts, the forest service wasn't able to meet the standards set by this designation; but as the district ranger stated, "It's finally our turn." Reconstruction has begun—replacing wood bars, doing rock work, building an elevated boardwalk and solving some of the flooding problems. In the future, a fee system may be implemented to maintain the recreation area, as well as the quality of the trail.

Roaring Run Trail begins with a history lesson. Hike through the picnic area (fork right) and take the bridge across Roaring Run Creek to the remains of an old iron furnace. Roaring Run Iron Furnace, which operated in the nineteenth century, is on the National Register of Historic Places. A pamphlet put out by the New Castle Ranger District describes it as a "standing pre-Civil War iron ore furnace, used for making iron ingots, stoves, and other iron products for the building of America."

Interpretive boards detail how the furnace worked. The material explains the role that Roaring Run Creek played. In short, the creek drove the wheel, which powered the bellows, which forced air into the furnace so it would burn hotter and melt the iron.

Walk behind the furnace and pick up the trail, which climbs through a dense forest of white pine, hemlock, and birch to the high point (1,520 feet) of the hike. Be sure to take the left fork. A stone balcony affords a view of a distant cascade on Roaring Run before the descent to the creek and a trail junction. The waterfall is 150 yards straight ahead.

Roaring Run Falls, a striking thirty-foot waterfall, splashes down an abrupt rocky drop. After the falls, Roaring Run Creek races through the gap in a series of shallow cascades and rapids on its way to the James River via Craig's Creek.

To finish the loop by following the course of the creek, zig-zag back and forth across it utilizing three bridges. Back at the picnic grounds, spread out a feast on one of the tables right beside Roaring Run Creek.

Roaring Run Creek isn't a clear mountain stream. The headwaters are not in the mountains. The unusual white-green color of the water is caused by the fact that the creek originates in limestone country, situated on private farm land in an area called Rich Patch in Alleghany County. I have never seen water this color. I thought it was beautiful.

The creek is stocked with trout and offers "put and take" fishing. The district ranger said, "Opening day (in April) is a circus. There are usually about three hundred cars in the parking lot. It is not quality fishing, but you can catch a trout." I'd recommended avoiding this waterfall hike during the beginning of trout season.

Directions: From Clifton Forge, take VA 220 south through Irongate towards Eagle Rock. About 12 miles before Eagle Rock, turn right onto VA 615, travel 5.2 miles, and turn right onto VA 621. Go 0.9 miles up VA 621 to the 0.2-mile entrance road for Roaring Run Furnace on the left. This road ends at a parking area, the trailhead begins at the upper end.

6

Glasgow

With few amenities or accommodations, Glasgow doesn't attract the tourist crowd. The town's best attribute is location. The rural community of Glasgow sits on the western slopes of the Blue Ridge Mountains at the confluence of the Maury River and James River, sandwiched between Jefferson National Forest and George Washington National Forest.

Indians inhabited the Blue Ridge for hundreds of years before the first white settlers. In 1670, the main camp of the Monacan Indians was located near Glasgow. These Indians ruled the Blue Ridge from the north banks of the James River eastward. The first pioneers, mostly Scotsmen, came to the area in the 1730s. One such immigrant, Joseph Glasgow, was a descendant of the Earl of Glasgow; another early resident was John P. Salling. Benjamin Borden owned Glasgow's first piece of land, which subsequently became part of the Salling and Glasgow homesteads. The oldest house in town, built by Peter A. Salling, still stands.

Glasgow was the site of the first battle west of the Blue Ridge between the Iroquois and the early settlers. On December 18, 1742, a skirmish started a series of conflicts that lasted two years. With the Treaty of Lancaster, the Indians gave up the Shenandoah Valley, pushing the fighting with settlers further west.

A real estate boom hit the Shenandoah Valley in the 1890s. Like many towns, Glasgow was a product of this instant growth created by development companies. General Fitzhugh Lee and several other gentlemen who made up the board of directors for the Rockbridge Company built themselves a town.

The company bought land, mapped out lots, and encouraged businesses to move into the area. But like many boom towns the story of Glasgow's progress was short-lived, and included a power plant that never ran and a hotel that never opened.

Today, Glasgow is a quiet town with a population of just over one thousand. The town's 1.5 square miles supports one big company, a textile factory called Burlington Industries. Except for the bank and high school, few other facilities exist in Glasgow. But while the community offers little in the way of craft shops, art galleries, or museums, you can dine at the Crossing Restaurant or overnight in the Bed and Breakfast Inn at Balcony Downs Plantation.

Although Glasgow doesn't have its own tourist attraction, you can drive a few miles west to the Natural Bridge, an incredible limestone formation, 215 feet high and 90 feet across. A brochure states that the bridge "once was the summit of a large waterfall. During the one hundred million years Cedar Creek flowed, there were also subterranean passageways in the softer stone under the existing arch which eventually washed away leaving the harder rock of the structure you see now."

The Monocan Indians believed the bridge, a gift from the Great Spirit, helped their people escape from the Shawnee and Powhattans. A canyon interfered with the Indians' retreat, but after kneeling in prayer, a bridge appeared across the canyon. The Monocan Indians called this natural wonder "The Bridge of God."

Pick up a map when you arrive and walk the self-guided tour. You will learn about the U.S. president who first owned the Natural Bridge and you will see another U.S. president's initials carved in the rock. The Natural Village includes a hotel and dining room, a gift shop, the Natural Bridge Caverns, and a wax museum that depicts Shenandoah Valley history.

Travelers use Glasgow as a base when visiting the two national forests. Outdoor recreation opportunities abound just outside of town—picnicking, hiking, hunting, swimming, fishing, and boating. The

Panther Falls is popular with local college students who come for the swimming hole below the falls. U.S. Forest Service photo.

Appalachian Trail leaves George Washington National Forest, crosses US 501, and enters Jefferson National Forest a few miles east of Glasgow.

Cave Mountain Lake, a national forest recreation area, opens in May and provides a bath house, picnic units, and camping through November. A lifeguard monitors swimming on the lake during the summer months. The beach is the length of a football field. Reasonable fees are charged for day and overnight use.

The 8,703 acres of the James Face Wilderness Area was the first designated wilderness area in Virginia. This special section of national forest, which only allows foot travel, provides for a primitive nature experience. Climb Highcock Knob (3,073 feet) to reach the highest elevation in the James Face Wilderness Area or hike along the James River (650 feet) to reach the lowest elevation. Balcony Falls Trail, a definite highlight, runs through part of the wilderness area starting from the parking lot at Locher Tract. Views from the ridgetop include the James River Gorge and the town of Glasgow.

The four waterfall hikes near Glasgow take you into both national forests. The two north of town wind through the Pedlar District of George Washington National Forest; the two south of town start on the Blue Ridge Parkway and drop into the Glenwood District of the Jefferson National Forest. So, pick up some picnic foods—a bucket of chicken and a side of slaw—at the corner grill in Glasgow and head for one of Virginia's national forests.

Fallingwater Cascades

1.6 mile loop, Moderate

Fallingwater Cascades is on a National Recreation Trail that was established, along with Flat Top Trail, in 1982. The trailhead is on the Blue Ridge Parkway, but you will enter the Jefferson National Forest (Glenwood District) within 50 yards. Stone steps lead down to Fallingwater Creek, and a footbridge signifies the beginning of the falls. The parking area is at 2,557 feet; the Cascades, 2,300 feet.

Fallingwater Creek originates on Chestnut Mountain and flows southwest to form the headwaters of Jenning's Creek. Located in the drainage for Wilkerson Gap, Fallingwater Cascades rushes 200 feet down the ridge. Two dead-end side trails, marked with signs, "150 feet to view," provide wonderful vantage points of the moderate-volume slide and the surrounding hemlocks and rhododendron.

Along the trail, you will find geologic formations called talus slopes, evidence of the weathering effect. Rock fragments detach from the mountainside and deposit at the base, creating a 40-degree slope that has a tendency to slide. Little, if any, vegetation grows here. The rock slopes on this hike open up incredible views of a mountain called Harkining Hill.

Fallingwater Cascades Trail is part of the Peaks of Otter Trail System. One mile into the hike, a trail off the loop to the right leads 40 yards up to a parking area for Flat Top Trail, a 4.5-mile trail connecting you to the picnic area at Peaks of Otter. The Peaks of Otter, a recreation area on the Parkway (between milepost 85.5 and 86), has a lodge, campground, and visitor center in addition to the picnic area. You can visit the Johnson Farm, a restored farm dating back to 1852, and get involved in the live demonstrations.

Directions: From Glasgow, take US 501 and travel 9 miles up to the Blue Ridge Parkway at the James River. Head south on the Parkway for 19.5 miles to Fallingwater Cascades Overlook on the right at milepost 83.1.

Apple Orchard Falls

2.4 miles roundtrip, Moderate

On the Blue Ridge Parkway stretch of the drive to Apple Orchard Falls, you will travel from the lowest point on the entire Parkway to the highest point on the Parkway in Virginia. The James River (elevation 668 feet) at milepost 63.7 is only thirteen miles from milepost 76.7 (elevation 3,950 feet) near Apple Orchard Overlook.

Apple Orchard Falls flows down the west side of Apple Orchard Mountain (4,225 feet), the second highest peak in Virginia. The orchards on Apple Orchard Mountain are really oak orchards, a form of northern hardwood forest that has been dwarfed by the extreme weather at this high elevation. The stunted northern red oaks and the lack of shrubs create "orchards" that are often mistaken for apples trees.

Although Apple Orchard Mountain doesn't have any apples, a few apple trees exist nearby. The gated road at the trailhead leads up to the former site of Camp Kewanzee, where a Cherokee Indian named Gus Welch ran a recreation area for travelers in the 1930s and 40s. The location has an orchard with a few apple trees.

Apple Orchard Falls Trail begins at Sunset Fields. The grassy clearing and excellent western view attract visitors who want to watch the sun go down. Hike to the falls in the late afternoon, timing your return to catch the sunset over the mountains.

The trail leaves park land and enters the national forest within the first 100 yards. From the parking area to the falls, the trail loses 1,000 feet in elevation. You'll intersect the Appalachian Trail and two old logging roads before reaching the creek. There is a footbridge at the brink of the falls, but you must cross the creek and do the switchbacks before being rewarded with a view.

The 150-foot Apple Orchard Falls, on a small tributary in the Parker Gap watershed, is part of the headwaters of North Creek. The tributary goes over several stair-steps before free-falling off a narrow overhang. At the base, it squeezes between huge boulders and flows into an isolated, open valley.

Instead of backtracking, try a one-way, downhill waterfall hike. Continue past the falls for 2.4 miles (another 1,000-foot elevation loss) to FSR 59. To set a shuttle car, take FSR 812 from the north end of Sunset Fields to FSR 768. Turn left and continue to FSR 59. The trailhead is to the left at the end of the road.

The area around Apple Orchard Falls Trail was once owned and logged by the Virginia Lumber and Extract Company. The forest service bought the land in 1917. A ceremony took place in October of 1987 to dedicate it as a National Recreation Trail.

In Glenwood District of Jefferson National Forest, Apple Orchard Falls is part of a special management area that protects the trail and surrounding drainage. This means no cutting! An estimated 500 acres is being set aside to emphasize recreation. Termed an "interior forest," the area is a nesting and breeding ground for song birds who winter in Central and South America.

Directions: From Glasgow, travel to the Blue Ridge Parkway at the James River (see directions under Fallingwater Cascades). Head south for 14.5 miles to Sunset Fields Overlook at milepost 78.4. The trailhead is in the middle of the parking area.

Staton's Falls

No hike necessary

Staton's Falls on Staton's Creek secured its name from a local family. William Staton of Amherst County, an early landowner in the area, may have owned property along the creek. Now the area around the falls is part of the Pedlar District of George Washington National Forest. Other names for Staton's Falls include Lace Falls and Deadman's Falls.

To portray Staton's Falls, I will share with you the words of Michael T. Shoemaker from his book *Hiking Guide to the Pedlar District*, because his description of the waterfall fits quite well. "It is composed of several falls and cascades, which when added together descend a great height. The interesting feature of Staton's Falls is not the height, however, but the distinctive zig-zag pattern of the series of falls."

Staton's Falls descends several hundred feet, and the first drop of fifteen feet is across the road from the parking area. An eighty-foot plunge follows immediately as the creek continues to crash through the gorge. Although a hike is not necessary to enjoy this waterfall, you may walk along the road for about 100 yards, scramble down the bank to the creek, and explore other cascades. Your opportunity for adventure here is as extensive as your energy. About one mile from the falls, Staton's Creek flows into the Pedlar River.

While driving on Fiddlers Green Way to Staton's Falls, about a half mile before you reach the parking area, there is a small pull-off on the left. Two posts indicate the spot where there used to be an interpretive sign entitled "Virgin Forest." Rangers suspect that a fraternity was responsible for stealing the sign.

The interpretive sign designated an area of "virgin," or old growth forest. Turn-of-the-century logging bypassed this small stand of trees because of the steep hillsides along Staton's Creek. This remnant of ancient forest is used as a research plot to monitor old growth. You will find yellow poplar, red oak, white pine, and hemlock. Some of the huge trees measure five feet around and one hundred feet tall.

Directions: From Glasgow, take US 501 to Buena Vista, where you'll find the office for the Pedlar Ranger District. Pick up US 60 and head east for 5 miles up to the Blue Ridge Parkway. Continue east on US 60 for 3.2 miles, where you'll see a sign for Oronco and SR 605 (Pedlar River Road). Turn left and travel 1.7 miles to a fork. Go right onto SR 633 (Fiddlers Green Way), which immediately turns to gravel. The parking area is 1.1 miles up SR 633 on the right. Walk across the road to the beginning of the falls.

Panther Falls

1 mile roundtrip, Easy

Panther Falls is on the Pedlar River in the George Washington National Forest. The waterfall's name reveals a time when panthers (often called mountain lions) roamed these parts. It would seem, the river's name recalls a time when peddlers roamed these parts, too. In his book, *Hiking Guide to the Pedlar District*, Michael T. Shoemaker states that this isn't so. He wrote, "Although peddlers were common along the Pedlar River, the river's name derives from the surname of an early settler who drowned in it." And he states, "The name of the Pedlar River was in use at least as early as 1742."

Panther Falls is often more a party place than a scenic area because the spot is popular with students from local colleges—even though alcohol is not permitted. The swimming hole below the falls is the primary attraction, and people dive off the boulders surrounding the pool. At certain points the water is over twenty feet deep, but a sign warns of submerged rocks. Several people have lost their lives here, and the sign states the date of the last death as well as a warning of strong currents and undertow.

In March, while the tail-end of winter blew snow flurries into my face, I was alone at Panther Falls and it was beautiful. The Pedlar River comes around an S-turn and creates an eight-foot wide chute where the river squeezes between two huge boulders. This powerful sluice falls ten feet into a blue-green pool before sliding over a smaller drop. The forest around the falls is second- and third-growth—about seventy years old.

On the drive to Panther Falls, after turning onto FDR 315A, you will pass Robert's Creek Cemetery, one of many old family cemeteries in the Pedlar District. The cemeteries mark "home places" from the pioneer days. Rock piles, terraces, and cleared land show evidence of farming from the late 1700s until the Depression.

Before you reach the gate to begin your hike, a path leads off to the right into a wildlife clearing. Created to add diversity to the woods and attract wildlife, this forest opening offers wonderful, primitive camping.

In addition, camping is allowed 150 yards from the river. (Yellow-diamond markers attempt to delineate this boundary.)

Begin your hike at the gate. The road was closed to vehicles in the mid-1980s because of overuse. A gradual descent on the roadbed takes you down to the Pedlar River. Signs tacked on trees read "Trout Fishing Waters." The Pedlar River, stocked several times in the spring (and in the fall if the water level cooperates), offers "put and take" fishing. Since the road to the falls was closed, the grasses and plants have slowly been restored in the large, open area. Follow the river a short distance to the falls.

Directions: From Glasgow, travel to the Blue Ridge Parkway via Buena Vista (see directions under Staton River Falls) and continue east on US 60. Just past the Parkway, turn right onto FDR 315, a well-graded gravel road. Travel 3.4 miles and turn left onto 315A, a 0.5-mile side road that ends in a parking circle. The trailhead is beyond the wooden information board at the lower end of the parking lot. The trail begins down the old roadbed past the gate.

Upper Cascades is the most accesible waterfall in Hanging Rock State Park. Photo by Nicole Blouin.

7

Hanging Rock State Park

ocated in one of the eastern-most mountain ranges in North
Carolina, Hanging Rock State Park spreads over 6,000 acres
of Surry and Stokes Counties. The Park lies in the Sauratown
Mountains, which take their name from the Saura Indians, thought to
be the area's earliest inhabitants. Archaeological evidence indicates that
there was a large Saura village near the confluence of Town Fork Creek
and the Dan River.

Locally known as "the mountains away from the mountains," the
Sauratown Mountains stand apart from their western neighbor, the Blue
Ridge Mountains. The Sauratown Range is a stunning sight, rising
above the adjacent terrain, which averages only 800 feet. Moore's Knob,
at 2,579 feet, is the highest point in the Park.

Hanging Rock State Park, as its name implies, has a unique
geological feature, the prominent outcrop of rock for which it was named.
The quartzite component of the mountains is largely responsible for this
protrusion. Over millions of years, this erosion-resistant mineral has
produced many impressive ridges and knobs called quartzite monad-
nocks. Other rocky precipices, which overlook the Piedmont Plateau and
the Dan River Valley, have descriptive names such as Indian Face, Wolf
Rock, Devil's Chimney, and Balanced Rock.

Over 300 species of flora have been identified in the Park. The forests
consist primarily of oak and pine, plus a mix of hickory, maple, tulip

trees, and dogwoods. Other vegetation includes rhododendron, laurel, azalea, galax, and a large variety of ferns. The exposed rock supports mosses and lichens and a few flowering plants, such as lady's slipper and fire pink, grow in the cracks.

Gray foxes, skunks, bats, rabbits, raccoons, and white-tailed deer are among the mammals that call Hanging Rock "home." Reptiles include frogs, lizards, and snakes—plus the state's only population of the Wehrler's salamander. The lake is primarily stocked with two types of fish, bass and bream. And bird songs, by performers such as the warbler, sparrow, and wood thrush, are most noticeable in the late spring and early summer.

On April 20, 1936, Hanging Rock State Park was established with a donation of 3,096 acres of land to the state of North Carolina by the Winston-Salem Foundation and the Stokes County Committee for Hanging Rock. As recently as 1982, land has been added to the Park for resource preservation and recreation. The Civilian Conservation Corps is responsible for most of the construction in the Park that occurred between 1935 and 1942, including a dam and twelve-acre lake, a picnic area and park road, and hiking and horse trails.

Hanging Rock State Park is open year-round. Family cabins are available by reservation from March through November. The Park also has a first-come, first-served campground with 73 tent and trailer sites (no hook-ups). Each site has a grill, table, and tent pad. Bathhouses are located nearby. You'll need reservations for the eight wilderness group sites, which have pit toilets and water. The Park has two picnic grounds that provide sheltered areas, tables, fireplaces, grills, and restrooms.

Aside from camping and picnicking, Hanging Rock State Park offers many forms of recreation. Try the lake, the river, or the rocks.

At the lake, although private boats are not allowed, rowboats and canoes can be rented from the boat house during the summer. There is a protected swimming area with a sandy beach and diving platform. Facilities include a restroom, a refreshment stand, and a lounge area with a magnificent view.

On the Dan River, there is boat-ramp access just north of the Park's main entrance. The Dan River is ideal for canoeing and tubing, and fishermen can spend a day trying their luck with small-mouth bass and catfish. A North Carolina fishing license is required.

For experienced rock climbers, climbing is permitted on the rocks. Cook's Wall and Moore's Wall provide a series of cliffs ranging up to 200 feet in height. All other areas are closed to climbing. Climbers must register prior to climbing and use proper equipment and saftey techniques.

The best way to get to know the Park is on foot. There are over eighteen miles of trails, most of which are connected. By hiking a total of only 3.5 miles, you can reach all five of the Park's waterfalls. The driving distance combined between the four trailheads only equals twelve miles. This makes it possible to see a lot of falls in a little time. Sound good?

Upper Cascades

0.6 miles roundtrip, Easy

Upper Cascades is the most accessible waterfall in Hanging Rock State Park. The wide gravel roadbed is considered feasible for handicapped people with assistance.

On the way to the falls, there is a superb mountain view from an outcrop of rock that overlooks Cascades Creek. The trail continues down to a well-built wooden deck with three levels. Steps lead down from the platform to the edge of the creek.

The near-vertical Upper Cascades flows over a rocky drop, which is ten feet wide by forty feet high. After sliding into a small pool below the falls, the stream squeezes through a gap between boulders and disappears. If you want to find out where the water goes, walk back out to the gravel, take a sharp left, and go down a steep, 30-foot grade to a ledge.

Downstream from the falls, after a series of short drops, Cascades Creek heads for Lower Cascades, which must be accessed separately, and eventually flows into the Dan River. Upstream from the falls, a dam (built in 1938) on Cascades Creek impounds the twelve-acre recreational lake.

The Cascades Gorge, like many steep ravines, escaped much of the logging in the 1930s. Some of the oldest trees in the Park, including giant hemlocks, can be seen below Upper Cascades.

The trail to Upper Cascades is one of the hikes that rangers often use for weekly summer interpretive programs. Waterfall hikes can also be set up by request for school, church, and other groups.

Directions: From the Park entrance, travel 1.7 miles on the main road and turn left at the sign that indicates Hanging Rock Trail. There is a large parking area. The trailhead is at the lower end of the parking area and is marked with a wooden sign.

Lower Cascades

0.6 miles roundtrip, Easy

Lower Cascades is the tallest and most spectacular waterfall in Hanging Rock State Park. It is on Cascades Creek, roughly two miles downstream of Upper Cascades. A series of thirty-foot slides combine for a total drop of 120 feet.

The waterfall is at the northern boundary of the Park in a ninety-one acre section between Hall Road and Moore's Spring Road. This land became part of Hanging Rock in 1974 when it was bought from a local medical doctor, Spotswood Taylor, who owned several pieces of property adjacent to the Park.

The refreshment stand at the lake sells postcards of Lower Cascades. The text on the back states that a Moravian botanist, Lewis David von Schweinitz, supposedly discovered the falls. Known as "the father of American mycology," Schweinitz also discovered approximately 1,500 species of plants near Hanging Rock and in the surrounding area.

The trail to Lower Cascades is the only one in the Park that doesn't connect to the other trails. A wide gravel roadbed leads you to the edge of a huge cliff where you stand one hundred feet above the gorge. The waterfall is almost directly beneath you. There are a few spots on the rocky ledge where the waterfall is visible only if you lean over the shelf.

North of the falls, on Moore's Spring Road, resorts developed at the turn of this century to take advantage of two mineral springs. Until the late 1920s, Piedmont Springs and Moore's Springs were popular destinations for those seeking the natural spring water.

Directions: From the Park gates, leave the Park and turn left on Moore's Spring Road. Take another left after 0.3 miles onto Hall Road. Go 0.4 miles to the parking area for Lower Cascades on the right. The trailhead is at the upper end of the parking area and is marked with a brown sign.

Waterfalls on Indian Creek

Hidden Falls: 0.8 miles roundtrip, Easy
Window Falls: 1.2 miles roundtrip, Moderate

Hidden Falls and Window Falls are on Indian Creek Trail, part of the Mountains-to-Sea Trail. The section of trail beyond Window Falls was completed in 1987 by volunteers and park employees. Now you can continue past the waterfalls, following the white blazes, for three miles along and across Indian Creek to the Dan River.

For a triathalon (hike, paddle, and sightsee!), arrange for a canoe to meet you at the Dan River parking area accessed from SR 1487, and a shuttle car to be parked at the public boat-ramp at Hemlock Golf Course. Hike the 3.7-mile Indian Creek Trail and paddle the 12.9-mile stretch of the Dan River. Sightseeing? Oh yes, stop along the river at Moratock County Park and visit the "Giant Fireplace," an iron smelting furnace built in 1843.

To begin the hike, walk the wide path through the picnic area and gradually descend to a fork (right). This short spur leads to Hidden Falls. After returning to the main trail and passing good views of Hanging Rock, the trail deteriorates somewhat and becomes rocky and steep before arriving at Window Falls.

Hidden Falls is nestled in a cove thick with rhododendron. Indian Creek flows over two short ledges, free-falls seven feet, and then slides another four to form this fifteen-foot waterfall.

Window Falls is a scant curtain of water that spills over an undercut ledge and splatters on the rock below. You can walk backstage, behind the twenty-foot curtain, and only get slightly wet. The waterfall is named for the "window" in the huge overhanging rock cliff just upstream. Crawl through the hole and discover... well, I guess I shouldn't give everything away!

Directions: From the Park entrance, follow the directions to the large parking lot (see directions under Upper Cascades). The trailhead is marked by a sign at the upper end.

Tory's Den Falls

0.6 mile roundtrip, Moderate

Tory's Den Falls was named for a Revolutionary War legend: a thirty-foot cave—Tory's Den—near the waterfall. As with many legends, the story changes with the storyteller, but all the old tales involving Tory's Den describe the cave as a refuge for loyalists.

I like to share the story about C. Jack Martin's daughter. Martin was a member of the Whig party who lived about fifteen miles from the cave during this era. His daughter was captured by the Tories, held for ransom, and hidden in the cave. Whether she was rescued because smoke was seen coming from the cave or a piece of material was found from her torn petticoat, the legend has a happy ending.

From Tory's Den Trail, you can visit the cave or the waterfall. Follow the narrow path, which is marked with plastic blue dots that are tacked onto trees. You will come to a sign that indicates Tory's Den is to the right (descend one hundred yards to the cave) and Tory's Den Falls is to the left (about twenty-five yards).

Tory's Den Falls is a delicate waterfall. A tiny creek spills over a series of rock terraces. The current is only five feet wide at the precipice, but then it divides and falls, and divides and falls again, getting wider with each drop. From where you stand, on the edge of a cliff opposite the main portion of the waterfall, you can see about thirty feet of Tory's Den Falls. Small trees and holly bushes are pushing up between rocks around the falls. The creek continues to drop on its way down the valley to the Dan River.

Directions: From the Park entrance, leave the Park and then turn left on Moore's Spring Road. Take another left after 0.3 miles onto Hall Road. Travel 2.4 miles to Mickey Road and turn left. After 0.4 miles turn onto Charlie Young Road and proceed 0.5 miles to a parking lot. The trailhead is marked with a wooden sign.

8

Stone Mountain State Park

For those who find the typical tourist scene in towns like Cherokee to be only slightly less terrifying than a terrorist attack, Stone Mountain State Park is the place to be. The friendly people in the remote, quiet counties of Wilkes and Alleghany are more oriented to serving fishermen, hunters and laid back farmers than they are towards tourism.

The Park, established in 1969, is home to the largest plutonic monadnock in the state. Defined in *The New Columbia Encyclopedia*, a monadnock is "an isolated mountain remnant standing above the general level of the land because of its greater resistance to erosion." Stone Mountain, a massive oval-shaped dome, rises 600 feet above the surrounding valley, its base stretching a lengthy four miles in circumference. Stone Mountain's elevation is 2,305 feet; its age, 360 million years.

There are countless backcountry adventures to be had at Stone Mountain State Park. The spectacular terrain makes the Park an appropriate place for a rewarding wilderness experience. No matter what your sport, Stone Mountain can help you enjoy solitude in the woods. Even during the hectic summer season between Memorial Day and Labor Day, the Park offers opportunities to escape.

One of the outdoor pursuits to be enjoyed in the Park is climbing. The granite exposures of Stone Mountain, along with Wolf Rock and Cedar Rock, provide a plethora of explored and unexplored routes—some of the best friction climbing in the South. During many months of the year, climbers can find solitude on the rock faces in the Park—a rarity in the South. You will need to check with the Park office, on the right as you enter the Park, to find out where climbing is permitted.

For fishermen interested in the elusive trout, there are almost twenty miles of brook fishing streams, which have been designated "trout waters." The native brook trout can sometimes be hooked. At the lower elevations, streams are regularly stocked with rainbow and brown trout.

The East Prong of the Roaring River is stocked by the North Carolina Wildlife Resources Commission, and during certain months natural bait can be used. There are two "fish for fun" streams in the Park—Bullhead Creek and Rich Mountain Creek. These streams are used to practice fly fishing and not to "catch and keep." Other creeks in the Park can be fished with single hook artificial lures. Check with the Park office for rules, regulations, and fees.

For campers, Stone Mountain provides thirty-seven family sites. All of them are relatively close to bathrooms, washrooms, and drinking water. Campsites are equipped with grills and picnic tables, with your choice of wooded or meadow sites. Individual sites are filled on a first-come, first-served basis; group sites (reservations needed) and backpacking sites (permit required) are also available. Fees are charged for all sites—individual, group, and backpacking. Stop at the Park office to find out about camping facilities.

Besides the intriguing rock faces, beautiful streams, and camping opportunities, Stone Mountain State Park has several historic points of interest. In addition to scattered chimneys, foundations, and old roadbeds, two buildings from the 1700s and 1800s still exist: the Hutchinson House and the Garden Creek Baptist Church.

The Hutchinson House, at the base of Stone Mountain, reminds us of the distinctive cabins built by the first settlers of the area. This cabin is not open to the public, but it is used occasionally for cultural programs. Restoration plans are in the works.

Jim Hutchinson turned loose domesticated goats in the 1940s, and six or seven of their descendants still reside under the ledge near the Great Arch. On occasion, these sure-footed feral goats parade along the exposed ridge of Stone Mountain and can be seen when viewing the south face.

The Garden Creek Baptist Church, built in the late 1770s, is still used even though the land is owned by the park service. A retired minister from Tennessee preaches on Sunday between mid-May and mid-October. The brief services are held earlier than regular church so the local folks can attend their own churches. Campers are welcome to attend the service.

As for the waterfalls, Stone Mountain State Park has four within its 13,378 acres. You can relax beside a waterfall after a long day of climbing, hiking, or fishing. You can camp near a waterfall, pitching a tent at one of the backpacking sites. And, most notably, you can visit a waterfall on your way to church!

Stone Mountain Falls

3.3 mile loop, Strenuous

R. Phillip Hanes, who donated over 1,000 acres to Stone Mountain State Park, saw some trash come down Stone Mountain Falls while he was on a picnic. In order to protect the falls, he decided to purchase them. The tract, which included the falls, was part of the first piece of land that Hanes bought in the area, but it was the last piece of land that he donated. Stone Mountain Falls became part of the Park in 1986.

The name of this waterfall shouldn't be a surprise, but it wasn't always Stone Mountain Falls. Old maps reveal other names, including Beauty Falls and Deer Falls. I like the story about the latter.

Sometimes deer who try to drink from Big Sandy Creek slip and crash over the falls to their death. Early residents saw opportunity instead of misfortune. Families were assigned different mornings to claim any deer at the base of the falls. Although a ranger assured me that the Park doesn't lose too many deer in this manner, I saw one at the edge of the pool on my visit.

Stone Mountain Loop Trail is your ticket to Stone Mountain View, Stone Mountain Falls, and the summit of Stone Mountain. The loop takes you through a valley and past the south face of the mountain. After entering the woods, you will hike a ridge to the falls. The last part of the trail takes you across the dome and down the other side to the parking area.

Stone Mountain View is a grassy meadow at the base of the south face. A plaque describes the dome as a registered natural landmark. Spread a blanket or relax on the bench. Watch the climbers struggle up routes with names like "Sufficiently Breathless" and "No Alternative," while wild goats effortlessly traverse the exposed sloping rock.

Stone Mountain Falls, a 200-foot sheet of falling water, slides down a near-vertical, broad granite slab. The falls are on Big Sandy Creek, which actually drops a total of 500 feet. Be sure to walk out to the pool at the base before starting the hike up the side of the waterfall.

Over 300 steps make up the elaborate staircase adjacent to the falls. Built in 1991, this man-made segment of trail ascends the east shoulder of Stone Mountain—alongside the falls and all the way to the top. Before the trail was improved, hikers went from tree to tree, climbing eroded switchbacks.

Controversy arose about this improvement. It seems some people didn't think a wooden staircase was particularly attractive in the woods. The park service claims the construction wasn't damaging. In fact, "it was quite a feat." Vegetation is now protected from the inevitable trouncing of visitor's footsteps.

You reach the summit of Stone Mountain (2,305 feet) about 2.7 miles into the hike, after a half-mile, steep incline. On top, there are sections of bare rock, lined on the edges with pine and cedar and sparsely covered with mosses and lichens. Follow the yellow blazes on the exposed rock. Look north to view the Blue Ridge and southwest to view Cedar Rock.

Directions: From the Park entrance, follow the main road for 2 miles to the large parking area on the left. A 0.6-mile, single-lane gravel road leads to a small picnic area—walk if you can because parking is limited to about 25 cars. When it is crowded, a ranger directs traffic. The trailhead is beyond the information board, at the base of the wooden staircase.

Middle Falls and Lower Falls

3.4 miles roundtrip, Moderate

When I headed off to visit Middle Falls and Lower Falls, my first question was "Where is the upper falls?" The answer: Upper Falls is yet another name for Stone Mountain Falls. All three waterfalls are on Big Sandy Creek. Middle Falls is about a half-mile downstream from Stone Mountain Falls. Lower Falls is about a half-mile downstream from Middle Falls.

Middle and Lower Falls are reached off the Stone Mountain Loop Trail on a side trail—an old roadbed that crosses Big Sandy several times (you may have to wade if the water's high). From the trailhead on Stone Mountain Loop Trail, walk 0.2 miles to a 0.1-mile spur (right) that leads to Middle Falls. Then return and continue 0.5 miles to Lower Falls, near the southern boundary of the Park. If you want to combine a hike to Middle and Lower Falls with the loop to Stone Mountain Falls, figure on a total of 4.9 miles.

Middle Falls is a series of small cascades, with one section that slides about thirty feet at a thirty degree angle into a large swimming hole. Lower Falls is similar, but somewhat steeper, sliding twenty-five feet over a smooth dome. Big Sandy narrows beyond the shallow pool; you can jump across the creek to a rock beach covered with colorful, palm-size stones.

Many youth programs bring their kids to Stone Mountain State Park and by-pass the recognized highlights—Stone Mountain Falls and the summit of Stone Mountain. Instead, they head for Lower Falls wearing old bathing suits or cut-offs. Sailing down the sliding falls is part of their "organized activity." I'm surprised Lower Falls doesn't have a more suitable name—Sliding Rock or Bust Your Butt Falls—like other natural water slides in the Blue Ridge.

Directions: From the Park entrance, travel the main road to the small picnic area at the trailhead for Stone Mountain Loop Trail (see directions under Stone Mountain Falls). The trailhead is 1.0 mile into the loop on the right where a wooden sign indicates Middle and Lower Falls.

Widow's Creek Falls

0.2 miles roundtrip, Easy

My husband and I were ready for a break after hiking the strenuous Stone Mountain Loop Trail. We were pleased to discover the thirty-foot Widow's Creek Falls a short distance off the road on a flat trail. Even though the hike to the falls is short, you can extend your visit by continuing on Widow's Creek Trail to one of six (A-F) backpacking sites. Site A is 1.5 miles upstream of Widow's Creek Falls; site F, 2.25 miles. On or near Widow's Creek, each primitive campsite accommodates four people and requires a permit and small fee.

Many stories attempt to account for the name "Widow's Creek." A friend of mine who lives in Winston-Salem explained, "At one time a string of widows lived near the creek." A ranger told me a tale about how at least one husband (a miner) could have died. He was panning for gold and fell off the falls while trying to retrieve the tools he'd lost in the creek.

Stone Mountain State Park owns all the watershed for Widow's Creek. The headwaters for Widow's Creek are just south of the Blue Ridge Parkway.

Widow's Creek, classified as a wild trout stream, is one of several streams in the Park that make up a total of seventeen miles of designated trout waters. To fish from Widow's Creek, you must use artificial lures with a single hook. The limit is four fish per day (minimum seven inches). Widow's Creek flows into the regularly stocked East Prong of Roaring River, which is classified as delayed harvest water.

Directions: From the Park entrance, follow the main road for 3.5 miles. (It becomes gravel just past the main parking area after 2 miles.) Pull over just past the bridge on either shoulder.

9

Blowing Rock

Blowing Rock claims to be one of the oldest resort areas in the Appalachians—"a destination resort since 1889." The town, developed in the 1880s, continues to serve summer residents and vacationers. Located at milepost 219.9, Blowing Rock is considered one of the few full-service communities along the Blue Ridge Parkway.

This charming village offers the highest quality shops, foregoing the typical tourist fare. The windows on Main Street reveal antiques, fancy gifts and expensive clothing. To add to the shopping experience, the second Saturday of each month between May and October, Blowing Rock hosts its famous "Art in the Park" on the village square. Highlighting over a hundred exhibits, this juried show brings out the best in southern art and crafts.

The town's namesake, The Blowing Rock, is an enormous cliff towering thousands of feet above the John's River Gorge. The rock walls create a unique formation in which northwest winds blow upward, returning light objects to the place from which they were thrown. This mysterious phenomenon even causes snow to fall "upside down." Scientific explanations aside, let's recount an Indian legend about two young lovers—a Chickasaw maiden and a Cherokee brave.

Wandering blissfully through the mountains, the two found themselves atop the Blowing Rock. The sky turned a deep blood red—a sign to the brave that his homeland was in danger. Torn between his pleading lover and his obligation to help his people, the brave leapt from the cliff to certain death. The heartbroken maiden prayed to the Great Spirit. And after many days, against a backdrop of another dark red sky, a great gust blew the brave back into her arms. Ever since, the winds at the Blowing Rock have swept upward from the gorge.

You don't have to be in love with a Cherokee brave to enjoy the wonders at the Blowing Rock. Located on US 321 a mile south of town, this attraction opens in April and usually closes in mid-November when High Country weather turns bad. Beyond the gift shop, a short gravel trail leads to an amazing overlook where winds blow strongly. Look southwest to sight Hawksbill Mountain and Table Rock; west to view Mt. Mitchell, the highest peak in the East, and Grandfather Mountain, the highest peak in the Blue Ridge.

Blowing Rock boasts several sites that appear on the National Registry of Historic Places. Take the Parkway south to visit the historic Moses H. Cone Manor House, located on Flat Top Mountain at milepost 294. The Cone Manor, once the summer home (twenty rooms!) of an industrialist and his family, opens in May and closes at the end of October (no admission fee). The beautiful grounds, stretching for 3,500 acres, consist of fishing ponds, old apple orchards and miles of hiking and horse trails. The impressive estate houses arts and crafts of the Southern Highland Handicraft Guild and continual artist demonstrations.

Other places on the National Registry include the Westglo Spa, now an all-inclusive resort, which was built by portrait painter Elliot Dangerfield and remained a private home for decades; and the Greenpark Inn, presently owned by Alan and Pat McCain, which has been in operation since the 1880s. The most recent addition to the Registry in Blowing Rock is the Village Cafe.

Although Blowing Rock boasts a quaint main street and attractions featuring Indian legend and industrialist wealth, there are two fun tourist traps of the regular type north of town on US 321/221. Tweetsie Railroad provides western-style entertainment with food and crafts galore. Theme park rides include the three-mile train excursion on the same steam engine used for transporting settlers at the turn of the century. Mystery Hill Entertainment Complex—actually several attractions in one location—provides a range of activities from a museum (circa 1903) to hands-on adventure, complete with a working radio station and the opportunity to stand inside a soap bubble.

As far as waterfalls are concerned, Blowing Rock offers something especially unique—a set of three falls practically in downtown. So after enjoying "Art in the Park," you can swing around the corner and take a hike. Of course, the other two waterfalls near Blowing Rock—Boone Fork and the Cascades—should not be overlooked. Located on the Blue Ridge Parkway, both waterfall hikes provide the superb scenery and excellent trail conditions that the recreation areas in the Park are known for.

Waterfalls on the Glen Burney Trail

New Year's Creek Cascades: 0.4 miles roundtrip, Moderate
Glen Burney Falls: 1.2 miles roundtrip, Moderate
Glen Mary Falls: 1.8 miles roundtrip, Strenuous

When you ask a local for directions to a waterfall, the answer is almost never "downtown." Well, Glen Burney Trail is just off Main Street in Blowing Rock; and from the trailhead at a town park, you can hike to three falls.

The park is actually a garden. You can walk the cedar path, which is lined with plants such as lamb's ear, borage, and wild strawberries, out to the wooden boardwalk that lies adjacent to New Year's Creek. This peaceful place is called Annie Cannon Park.

The town owned a half acre and the Cannon Family gave $100,000 to develop it into a park. Annie Ludlow Cannon, wife of J.W. Cannon of Cannon Textile Industry, taught Sunday school for years and did extensive social work, helping start the Community Club and supporting the Grandfather Home for Children. She was a true friend to the town of Blowing Rock.

Blowing Rock has had many friends; and another one of note is Emily Puruden, a school teacher who donated the land around the waterfalls to be preserved as part of the Park. At the turn of this century, she started the Skyland Academy, a boarding school for underprivileged children. There is a marker at the south end of town (junction of US 321 business and by-pass) that commemorates her benevolence.

The Glen Burney Trail is not new. Old-timers say it's been around as long as they can remember—over a hundred years. You can pick up a free map of the Glen Burney Trail at the Chamber of Commerce.

After passing the sewage pump station and Dock Side Iris Restaurant, the trail descends into the Glen Burney Gorge. There are some ruins from the early 1920s of a non-mechanical, gravity-flow waste water plant that served the Mayview Manor Hotel, which was torn down in 1978. For its time, the plant was extremely sensitive to the environment.

At the Cascades, a wooden bridge crosses New Year's Creek and provides a place to sit and dangle your feet over this scant slide. A picnic table indicates you're near Glen Burney Falls. Walk 100 yards to the observation deck at the brink and enjoy looking out over the John's River Gorge. Farther on, there is a longer side path that will take you to the bottom of Glen Burney Falls. The trail weakens near the last and largest waterfall, Glen Mary Falls, but a rocky outcropping affords a nice view.

Directions: In downtown Blowing Rock, turn off Main Street onto Laurel Lane. At the four-way stop (Wallingford Street), continue straight. Just before the bridge, turn left into Annie Cannon Park. The trailhead is just beyond the information board.

Boone Fork Falls

5 mile loop, Strenuous

There are several books that detail this loop, but twenty-five-foot Boone Fork Falls always gets just a mention. Even though it is a pretty cascade, the falls gets upstaged by a creek with a celebrated name, a virgin forest that was cut by one famous person and bought by another, and a trail that is one of the best along the Blue Ridge Parkway.

The falls are on Boone Fork, which was named after Daniel Boone's nephew, Jesse. He had a cabin and a small farm near the creek in the early 1800s. A huge tract of virgin chestnut, poplar, and hemlock was forested

Cold, clear water splashing over rocks beneath a canopy of green makes a welcome sight on hot summer days. Photo by Joe Cook.

in the early 1900s by William S. Whiting, a great lumber baron. And Julian Price, founder of Jefferson Standard Life, one of the nation's major insurance companies, purchased the land in the late 1930s to use as a retreat for his employees. Price was killed in an automobile crash and the land was donated to the National Park Service. Boone Fork was dammed to form Price Lake, a memorial to a man who deeply loved these parts.

Julian Price Park, one of the most popular recreation areas on the Parkway, was dedicated in 1960. It consists of 4,200 acres of mountain land, ranging in elevation from 3,400 to 4,000 feet. There is a campground, picnic area, and a lake with boat rentals.

If you travel the Boone Fork Loop counterclockwise, you will first walk through an ancient lake bed where rich soil supports strawberries, blackberries, wild mustard, and pink roses. The field is great for bird-watching! Then, you will pass some rock outcroppings with several caves that provided shelter for pre-historic Indians. *Note:* 100 yards past the unusual wooden ladder, head right and back towards the river.

The trail parallels Boone Fork—watch for wood ducks and evidence of energetic beavers. The waterfall is at 1.8 miles. From the guardrail, thirty feet above the creek, you can see Boone Fork rushing and falling over car-sized boulders.

After the falls, the trail heads away from Boone Fork and follows Bee Creek, which you cross more than a dozen times on the way up to its headwaters. Then, there is a steep climb up a set of wooden stairs. During the last mile, you hike through open meadow, high above the two creeks, and through a section of the campground.

Directions: Leave downtown Blowing Rock heading south on US 221. Travel 1.7 miles to an entrance for the Blue Ridge Parkway on the right. Get on the Parkway and head south (left) for 1.8 miles. Julian Price Park will be on the right at milepost 296.4. Park near the restrooms. There is a brown forest service sign just beyond the building directing you across Boone Fork Creek to the trailhead at the information board and map.

Cascades

1.2 mile loop, Moderate

"Water...like liquid lace from overhead...dashes past to swirl and slide downward in an abandon of spray and foam ripples." The quote is from a plaque near the top of the Cascades, and it is an accurate description because the narrow, fifty-foot waterfall rolls and rushes past you, rather than falling at your feet. The waters from Falls Creek are bound for the ocean at Winyoh Bay, South Carolina, after flowing into the Yadkin River, which in turn flows into the Pee Dee River.

The Cascades Nature Trail is what the Blue Ridge Parkway calls a self-guided trail. There are metal plaques along the way providing information about the flora. You will learn when flowers bloom, where certain plants live, and which trees the mountaineers used for what—knowledge you can carry with you on any waterfall hike in the Blue Ridge.

To follow the loop counterclockwise, bear right at each of the forks. The trail follows Falls Creek through a dense hardwood forest, crosses the creek on a wooden bridge near the top of the Cascades, then heads down a well-built walkway that hugs the side of the waterfall. The upper platform is at the brink, the lower platform is half-way down. Retrace your steps up the stairs and look for the sign "Return Trail."

The Cascades is at E.B. Jeffress Park, 600 mountainous acres honoring a man who loved this land. Jeffress was chairman of the North Carolina highway department in the early 1930s; he fought hard in favor of building the proposed Blue Ridge Parkway through North Carolina.

Directions: From downtown Blowing Rock, follow Main Street (US 321 business) north to where it intersects with US 321 by-pass. Turn left (north) and travel for about 1.5 miles to the Blue Ridge Parkway. Head north on the Parkway. You will see a sign indicating that Jeffress Park is 19 miles away (at milepost 271.9). The trailhead is just beyond the restrooms.

10

Linville

On July 4th of 1892, the Eseeola Inn, located in the Linville Valley, celebrated its grand opening with a spectacular gala. Except for some farms, this stately mansion, with dignified guests and fancy cuisine, stood alone at the foot of Grandfather Mountain.

It all began with the vision of town builder Samuel Kelsey. Ten years earlier, Kelsey founded the town of Highlands. He wanted to create another "Highlands" in this valley because he found the "magic" here that originally drew him to the area of present-day Highlands.

The Linville Company was organized. The president, Donald MacRae from Wilmington, presided over the first meeting and then turned the enterprise over to his son. The job called for a younger man. Donald MacRae died shortly after the hotel opened.

Several years after the hotel's grand opening, a golf course was built—designed by Donald Ross. It is considered the first golf course in the mountains of North Carolina. The rest is a story of a growing and properous mountain resort. And Linville is a beautiful resort town, quaint and small, with little commercialism.

One of the historic buildings in Linville, The Old Hampton Store, operates the only grist mill in the area. When the Depression hit, Mr. Hampton settled with the locals who brought in herbs by giving them wooden coins that could be used in his community store. Stop in and browse, and don't pass up the pancake mix and corn meal.

Grandfather Mountain, the most dominant physical feature in Linville and the highest peak in the Blue Ridge, was named for the outline of a bearded man looking up towards the sky. Grandfather, whose rocky formations are 140 million years old, stands watch over this summer resort from an elevation of 5,194 feet. The Indians first called him "Tanawha," meaning fabulous hawk or eagle, for the great birds that soar above his head. Look for his "profile" from NC 105 in Foscoe, about seven miles north of Linville.

Grandfather resides in a 4,000-acre wilderness preserve that is open daily except Thanksgiving and Christmas. At this privately owned park, you can visit the famous Mile-High Swinging Bridge, which stretches 228 feet between two peaks (or two features of Grandfather's face) and the Environmental Habitat, which houses bear, deer, eagles, and cougars.

In addition, the recently opened Nature Museum, which includes a gift shop, restaurant and movie theater, offers over two dozen exhibits on mountain plants, wildlife, and minerals. Or go hiking. Bring a picnic and pick up a hiking permit for $4 at the entry gate. Be sure to ask for the free trail map. Grandfather's fourteen miles of trail include two National Recreation Trails.

Check the calendar of events for Grandfather Mountain, which lists happenings such as photography workshops and musical concerts. In July at Mckae Meadows near the base of Grandfather Mountain, you will find huge crowds (close to 20,000 people) enjoying a Scottish festival that goes well beyond plaids and bagpipes. The Grandfather Mountain Highland Games, considered this country's best highland games, is the annual gathering of over a hundred Scottish clans.

This outdoor event begins with a traditional torch-bearing ceremony, and the following days provide visitors with the opportunity to trace their heritage back to its original clan, listen to music performances, and watch national and international championship dancing. Sporting events include tossing sheaves and cabers, a traditional track and field meet, and the most difficult marathon in America, which follows a stretch of the Parkway.

A shop called Everything Scottish Shop, located on NC 105 in Foscoe, can provide information about the games. Posters and flyers concerning the event are up by March.

We've taken you to the top of Grandfather Mountain, and to the bottom, but a famous bridge "not to be missed" will take you along a piece of Grandfather's girth. The Linn Cove Viaduct, a missing link of the Blue Ridge Parkway, was completed in 1983 after years of battles between the park service and private individuals. The environmental issue was one of the loudest concerns. Figg and Muller Engineers provided the answer by creating a design and construction method—a huge S-shaped, elevated road—that wouldn't damage the sensitive nature of the rocky Linn Cove.

The Viaduct, considered the most complicated structure of its kind, took four years to build and cost $10 million. Visit this remarkable, 1,243-foot bridge at milepost 304.6. The folks at the visitor center (south end of the Viaduct) can provide more history and answer your questions.

Don't limit your visit in the Linville area to Grandfather Mountain. Head south for seven miles on US 221 to Humpback Mountain, where two explorers, H.E. Colton and Dave Franklin, discovered a cave in the early 1800s. During the Civil War, deserting soldiers hid out here.

Today, Linville Caverns is open year-round (weekends only in the winter). Two hundred feet below ground, the Caverns remain a constant fifty degrees. Visitors are guided on a forty-minute tour to see colorful formations such as the Frozen Waterfall and the Franciscan Monk. In addition, an underground stream supports blind trout. Hundreds of years of living without light caused many of the fish to lose their ability to see.

Two other mountains of note include Sugar Mountain and Mill Ridge, and the key word here is "winter." Both mountains offer skiing for all levels. Sugar, located on NC 184 one mile from NC 105, provides eighteen slopes and exquisite slopeside lodges, condos, and chalets. Mill Ridge, located on NC 105 just north of town, provides economy skiing on its five slopes.

Enough about mountains. What about the falls around Linville? Well, the following waterfall hikes involve more than just a parking area and a trailhead. Visiting Linville Falls, Dugger Falls and Elk Falls will lead you to two wonderful recreation areas, complete with camping and picnicking facilities. Stay awhile!

Linville Falls

Falls Trail: 1.6 miles roundtrip, Easy
Gorge Trail: 1.4 miles roundtrip, Strenuous
Plunge Basin Trail: 1 mile roundtrip, Moderate

Instead of several waterfalls on one trail, Linville Falls Recreation Area offers three trails to one waterfall with a total of six different views. Hosting about 50,000 visitors annually, Linville Falls is probably the most famous waterfall in the Blue Ridge. It was designated a Natural Heritage Area in 1989.

Linville Falls is a double cascade with a vanishing act between the two falls. The upper falls is wide and gentle, pouring over several shelves for a total of fifteen feet. Here, the river is lazy.

Suddenly, the river disappears into a narrow, quartzite channel. Out of sight, it dives sixty feet through a winding chamber before reappearing as the lower falls, a thunderous forty-five foot drop. The force of this powerful river has shaped a large basin with towering cliffs. The river flows out of the pool, leaves the recreation area, and enters the Linville Gorge Wilderness Area.

The headwaters of the Linville River are on Grandfather Mountain, and the river flows to the Catawba Valley through one of the most rugged gorges in the country. The sheer rock walls of Linville Mountain (west) and Jonas Ridge (east) confine the water for twelve miles while it descends two thousand feet. The difference in elevation between the rim and river is about fifteen hundred feet.

The Cherokees called the area "Eeseeoh," which meant river of cliffs. Settlers called the river and the falls "Linville" to honor the explorer William Linville, who in 1766 was attacked and killed in the Gorge by Indians.

In 1952, John D. Rockefeller donated the cascade tract to the National Park Service. The 440-acre recreation area offers picnic sites, a

This view of the lower falls is from Chimney View on the Linville Falls Trail. Photo by Frank Logue.

small bookstore, and a park service campground with a camp store. Rangers conduct interpretive programs, including campfire talks and guided nature walks; and an information shelter provides a large map of the trail system directing you to the Falls Trail, the Gorge Trail, and the Plunge Basin Trail.

The Linville Falls Trail is the most popular route to view the falls. There are four overlooks along the rim of the gorge that present a variety of perspectives: First Overlook (upper falls), Chimney View (the chimney-shaped rock for which it was named and the first look at the lower falls), Gorge View (the river cutting through the mountains), and Erwins View (the spectacular gorge and a distant view of the falls).

The Linville Gorge Trail is my favorite because it goes to the bottom, face to face with this magnificent waterfall. Only from the river's edge can I fully appreciate the grandeur of any gorge.

The Plunge Basin Trail, which descends about one-third of the way into the basin, is the shortest route to view the lower falls. This unusual overlook is a rocky platform jutting out from the hillside—like balcony seats at a great performance.

Directions: Leave Linville and head south on US 221 to Pineola. Take NC 181 heading south for about 2 miles and access the Blue Ridge Parkway on the left. Travel south to milepost 316.5 and turn left onto the 1.4-mile spur road that leads to Linville Falls Recreation Area.

Duggers Creek Falls

0.3 mile loop, Easy

"Our minds, as well as our bodies, have need of the out-of-doors. Our spirits, too, need simple things, elemental things, the sun and the wind and the rain, moonlight and starlight, sunrise and mist and mossy forest trails, the perfumes of dawn and the smell of fresh-turned earth and the ancient music of wind among the trees."—Edwin Way Teal.

This is one of several quotes you will encounter on Duggers Creek Loop Trail, an interpretive walk into a smaller version of Linville Gorge.

Other nature writers, such as John Muir, will meet you in the woods with thoughtful words of inspiration.

From a wooden bridge, you can look upstream and view Duggers Creek Falls, one of the smallest named falls in the Blue Ridge. The creek flows through a narrow chute as it enters the tiny canyon and spills over a ten-foot ledge. The rock walls are fifteen feet apart at the bridge, only three feet apart at the falls. Duggers Creek flows down Jonas Ridge and into the Linville River.

The trail begins in a tunnel of rhododendron that leads you down to Duggers Creek. Cross on the wooden bridge, climb two short sets of stone steps, and immediately descend from the rocky area on gradual switchbacks. After a sharp left, cross the creek again (this time on boulders), and enjoy reading the last metal plaque before returning to the parking area.

Directions: Travel to Linville Falls Recreation Area (see directions under Linville Falls). Leave from the sidewalk on the right at the lower end of the parking lot, and head slightly up and into the woods.

Elk Falls

0.8 miles roundtrip, Easy

No one knows how deep the pool is at the bottom of this waterfall. The Elk River drops eighty-five feet over a wide, even ledge to form Elk River Falls and then crashes into a huge rock bowl that looks like an amphitheater. Divers going down with weights have not been able to fight the force pushing upward. There are several stories of bags of silver being dropped into the pool during the Civil War.

Like many place names in the mountains, the river and the falls honor the eastern elk, a great animal that inhabited the area when wild lands stretched across the southern Appalachians. A relic of the Ice Age, the elk was the largest member (weighing five hundred to one thousand pounds) of the deer family and was often confused with the moose. Elk, called "wapiti" by the Indians, were last seen in the Blue Ridge in the early 1800s.

There is a story about a woman who lived on the Elk River (about nine miles from the falls) but thought she was in Kentucky. It was 1825 when Delilah Baird of Valle Crucis eloped with Johnny Holtzclaw, who was supposed to take her to his property in Kentucky. Three years passed and one day when Delilah was out gathering ginseng, she found some of her father's cattle and discovered she was only eight miles from home. Delilah reunited with her family but then returned to her "Kentucky" home.

Elk Falls is located in Elk Falls Recreation Area, a wonderful place to spend a day. You can swim or fish, and there are picnic tables along the river above the falls. A few miles upstream, you'll find the Elk River Campground, which is a wonderful place to spend a night. You can fall asleep to river sounds at one of the fifty oversized sites.

Don, the owner of the campground, told me that trout fishing is good, the area is a bird sanctuary, and his pavilion has a fireplace that is set up for cooking. The campground is open year round.

Directions: Leave Linville and head north on NC 181 to Newland. At the first stop light, turn right onto NC 194 and travel 7 miles to Elk Park. About 0.2 miles north of town, turn right at the sign for the Elk River Campground; and after 0.3 miles, turn left onto Elk River Road. The campground will be on your left at 1.5 miles, and the pavement ends at about 2 miles. Follow the gravel road until it ends (another 1.5 miles) at Elk Falls Recreation Area. The trailhead is at the upper end of the parking area, up the wooden steps.

11

Little Switzerland

Little Switzerland looks like it sounds—a small piece of Switzerland in the mountains of North Carolina. The town was named for its similarity to areas in the Swiss Jura Mountains on the French-Swiss border. The village, filled with Swiss-style houses, literally clings to the side of a mountain. In keeping with the town's theme, the lodges and shops have names like Alpine Inn, Chalet Switzerland Inn, Edelweiss Shop, and Chalet Shopping Plaza.

Ten executives from Charlotte, searching for a cool summer retreat for their families, founded the community of Little Switzerland in 1910. They created the Switzerland Company, bought land, divided it into lots, and constructed roads and a water system.

The small mountaintop village of Little Switzerland, located at milepost 333.9, is one of the few towns that sits right on the Blue Ridge Parkway. One-half mile north on the Parkway, you can drive through a tunnel by the same name. The Little Switzerland Tunnel, the first in a series of twenty-five tunnels on the Parkway before Cherokee, North Carolina, stretches for 542 feet.

Although Little Switzerland's winters can't compare to those in the Alps, you can still have some fun when it snows. When the Parkway is closed to traffic, the stretch north to Linville Falls offers some of the best sledding and cross-country skiing in western North Carolina.

Geneva Hall, in the center of Little Switzerland, is the headquarters for many community happenings. The facility hosts artisans, lecturers, and musicians. Activities include everything from dances to bridge tournaments. You will find a list of events at the post office, and take time to talk to the area's friendliest postmaster about anything pertaining to Little Switzerland.

Little Switzerland is noted for its broad panoramas—mountain after mountain after mountain, as far as the eye can see. For one of the best vistas in town, drive up to the top of Clarkson Knob (4,000 feet). The mountain, originally called Grassy Mountain, was named for Justis Harriot Clarkson, the founder of the town. Most locals still refer to the knob by its former name.

From the top, you can see Grandfather Mountain, Table Rock, Hawksbill and the entire Black Mountain Range, including Mt. Mitchell. The glitter and twinkle of distant town lights make the view sensational at night, too.

If driving up a 1.5-mile, one-lane gravel road doesn't interest you, try Woody Knob—two miles north of town. Some residents consider it the "better view" because vegetation on Grassy Knob is "growing up."

Little Switzerland is also noted for Gillespie Gap. The National Historic Overmountain Victory Trail, which passes through Gillespie Gap (where the Parkway goes over NC 226), commemorates an historic march of the Revolutionary War. The Overmountain Men journeyed through Gillespie Gap on their way to South Carolina to fight Major Patrick Ferguson and his British army. The contest was the Battle of Kings Mountain; the date, October 1780; the outcome, a triumphant success for the American forces. Every year a group of men, women and children re-enact the march, stopping to camp at Gillespie Gap just as the Overmountain Men did over 200 years ago.

Above all else, Little Switzerland is noted for its location in one of the richest mineral districts in the country—the Spruce Pine Mineral District. Commercial mining has been an important part of this area for seventy years. At one time, over 400 mines operated in the district. Fifty-seven minerals, including emeralds, garnets, rubies, amethysts, and quartz, have been found here. As many as forty-five have been found in one mine!

The nearby town of Spruce Pine holds its annual Minerals Festival at the Pinebridge Coliseum in late July or early August. A retail show hosts approximately fifty dealers who put out their various wares. You can choose a gemstone and a piece of jewelry, and the artisans will cut and set your stone while you wait.

To learn more about the rocks and minerals in the state, visit the Museum of North Carolina Minerals, a Parkway concession at milepost 331. The ranger is always happy to answer questions. And don't miss the Emerald Village, the number one mining attraction in North Carolina. At this museum and underground mine, you can hunt for gems, tour a recreated mining town, watch gemstones being cut, and shop for gifts and antiques. The wonderful displays and interpretive information tell about conventional methods and equipment and about the history and heritage of miners.

Stop in at a local rock shop for directions to one of several commercial gemstone mines that are open to the public. Buy a bucket of mineral-rich ore and join the rockhounds. Just throw some dirt in your pan and wash it in the mine's flumes. If you come up empty, be assured that there are many other gems to be discovered—the waterfalls around Little Switzerland. And they may be easier to find!

Roaring Fork Falls

1 mile roundtrip, Easy

Roaring Fork is in the Toecane District of Pisgah National Forest and flows into the South Toe River. The trailhead is at the entrance to the Busick Work Center, a forest service work place that also houses tools and equipment.

Follow the old logging road and don't be alarmed when you pass some run-down brick buildings labeled "Danger" and "Explosives." They held dynamite, blasting caps, drills and jack hammers in the early 1950s when the forest service did their own road construction. Now that sort of work is contracted out.

Just before crossing Roaring Fork, a sign will direct you to the right. One hundred yards upstream of the wooden bridge, Roaring Fork Falls rushes thirty feet down a narrow, zig-zag slide.

Directions: From Little Switzerland, pick up the Parkway and head

Roaring Fork flows to the South Toe River. Photo by Nicole Blouin

south. Travel to milepost 344.1 and exit north onto NC 80. Drive north for 2.3 miles and turn left onto FS 472 (South Toe River Road), just before the Mt. Mitchell Golf Course. Take the first left (after 0.1 miles) at the sign indicating Roaring Fork Falls and Busick Work Center. The road dead-ends at the work center. Park near the gate on the right. There is a sign that says "Falls, 0.5."

Setrock Creek Falls

1.4 miles roundtrip, Easy

Setrock Creek Falls is located in Pisgah National Forest at the Black Mountain Recreation Area. In addition to the waterfall hike, you can ride on a bicycle trail, float down the South Toe River in an inner-tube, or climb Mt. Mitchell, the highest peak in the East, using the 5.6-mile Mt. Mitchell Trail.

The Black Mountain Campground, at an elevation of 3,000 feet, is open between April and October. The tent and trailer sites (no hook-ups) have tables, fire rings, grills, and lantern posts. Each group site can accommodate fifty people (reservations required). An amphitheater houses programs on weekend evenings.

On the way to Black Mountain Recreation Area and Campground, you'll pass the "Y" junction of Neal's Creek Road and FS 472. At one time, this was part of a state-owned wildlife refuge and a game warden issued permits. There was a fish hatchery stocked from the South Toe River, Neal's Creek and Curtis Creek. The area became forest service game land because the state made a land exchange for some acreage to be used as part of Mt. Mitchell State Park. Stop in the small stone building for brochures, maps, and books on the Blue Ridge—or a visit with the ranger.

Begin this waterfall hike by walking the gravel road for about 0.4 miles to a brown forest service stick marking the trail on the right. Head up five stone steps and into the woods. Don't cut towards the creek too early. When the trail widens and begins a steep ascent, fork left to reach the falls.

Setrock Falls has four distinct levels, each about ten feet high, for a total of fifty feet of falling water. The creek splashes over small boulders, then flows the short distance to the South Toe River.

Directions: From Little Switzerland, travel to FS 472 at the Mt. Mitchell Golf Course (see directions under Roaring Fork Falls). FS 472 becomes gravel after 0.8 miles, there are picnic tables on the South Toe River at 1.5 miles, and Neals's junction (take right fork) is at 2.0 miles. Turn right (0.6 miles from the fork) into the campground—over the river on a cement bridge—and go left toward Briar Bottom (the group campsite). Park in the small area on the right before the gate and begin hiking up the gravel road.

Crabtree Falls

2.5 mile loop, Moderate

Crabtree Falls is on Crabtree Creek accessed by Crabtree Loop Trail in Crabtree Meadows. No mystery behind where this place got its name! Flowering crabtrees were once plentiful, growing wild in the fields. Unfortunately, that was in the old days when, like the many apple orchards in the area, they were maintained and cared for. Only a few scattered trees remain, but each May, they announce themselves with attractive pink blooms.

Crabtree Falls, crowned with hemlock and cloaked in rhododendron, plunges sixty feet down a wide and even rock face. The moderate volume of the creek skips lightly over the little ledges. The royal carpet that spreads out before the falls displays showy, lily-like trillium.

Crabtree Creek turned a corn mill during the first half of the 1800s. The Penlands owned the property and Billy Bradshaw managed it, hiring locals to help with crops, livestock, and most importantly, the mill. The corn mill was the main source of income; families came from surrounding valleys to bring their corn to mill. Because the creek had a small-but-fast current, Billy used a tub mill. This type of mill was designed for mountain streams and turned horizontally instead of vertically.

Crabtree Falls Loop Trail is known for its wildflowers—more than forty species—including lady slippers, wild orchids, and jack-in-the-pulpits. The well-groomed gravel path leads down gradual switchbacks through an oak-hickory forest. You'll cross several wet-weather springs, where salamanders flourish, before reaching the base of the falls (0.9 miles) and a large, open hollow that is covered with ferns from end to end.

Cross the creek and begin the 1.6-mile return route, which is not as steep as backtracking. As you climb the moderate switchbacks, you are rewarded with a different view of the falls. Once you reach the ridge, the trail is more gentle, crossing the creek and several of its tributaries on split-log bridges. Keep left at any junction; signs will direct you back to the campground.

Crabtree Meadows is a 253-acre recreational area that lies at 3,740 feet in the shadow of the Black Mountains. Part of the Blue Ridge Parkway, its facilities include a gift shop, restaurant, gas station, amphitheater, and campground. The picnic grounds are separate—just south and across the road. Between May and October, the concessions are open and park rangers lead nature walks and give evening interpretive talks.

Directions: From Little Switzerland, pick up the Parkway and head south. Travel to milepost 339.5 and turn right into Crabtree Meadows Recreation Area, following the road to the campground information building, where you can pick up a park service map that gives an overview of the recreation area and trail. If the campground road is closed, you'll have to walk an additional 0.3 miles.

12

Marion

In McDowell County, twelve miles off the Blue Ridge Parkway, Marion lies in the Catawba River Valley—down the mountain, but still in the mountains. Located off a major interstate and on the edge of a national forest, Marion sits between the highway and the woodlands. Interstate 40 runs along the southside, linking you to Asheville or Morgantown without small-mountain-road driving. The woodlands—Pisgah National Forest—are home to the Ranger Office in Marion for the Grandfather District, which includes the Wilson Creek Area and the Linville Gorge Wilderness.

Much of Marion's past lies behind the walls of two historic buildings. The McDowell House and the Carson House reveal stories about the earliest settlers, the place names, and the found-ing of the county and the town.

The county was named for Joseph McDowell, the man who built the McDowell House which is located on US 70 just west of the junction with US 221. McDowell's notable role in the American Revolutionary battles at Kings Mountain and Cowpens made him a local hero. His father, a fine hunter who was called "Hunting John," originally settled in the valley during the 1750s.

The county was organized in March of 1893 inside the Carson House, located on US 70 west of the McDowell House just over the Catawba River. Now a registered historic site, the house was built in

1780 by Colonel John Carson, and was used first as the county seat. When the courthouse was built in 1845 and the county seat was moved, the Carson House operated as an inn and stagecoach stop, then a girl's school, and today a museum.

Two months after the founding of the county, Colonel Carson presented fifty acres to create the town of Marion. The town's name came from Francis Marion, the "Swamp Fox." A hero in the American Revolutionary War, Francis acquired the nickname for his sly, masterful skills in the backwoods.

The Carson House itself is interesting but not as fascinating as its occupants. Colonel John Carson married twice; the first time to Rachel McDowell, a daughter of "Hunting John" McDowell. They had seven children. Later, he remarried, this time to Mary, the widow of Joseph McDowell (his sister-in-law), and together they had five children.

Today the Carson House stands as a tribute to southern colonial life and contains memorabilia and furniture from that time period, as well as Carson family belongings. One room in particular is given over to the historical archives and genealogical records of the people of McDowell County and western North Carolina. The house is open for tours (small fee) in the afternoon from May through October.

While two old homes contain much of Marion's history, one lovely mountain lake creates the center for much of Marion's recreation. Between 1916 and 1923, Duke Power Company dammed the Catawba River, Paddy Creek and Linville River. The impounded water—Lake James—took its name from James B. Duke, the founder of Duke Power Company. This 6,510-acre developed lake rests at an elevation of 1,200 feet and boasts over 150 miles of shoreline.

In 1987, government-appropriated funds enabled approximately 550 acres of land around Lake James to be purchased and developed into the state's newest park. To reach the entrance for Lake James State Park, travel northeast on NC 126 for about five miles.

Recreational activities at Lake James State Park include camping, picnicking and water sports. The Park offers primitive campsites (several with water faucets) and a bathhouse. You can picnic along the shoreline or at a table with a grill. Skiing and fishing are obvious water-sport favorites, and a beach, complete with lifeguards and a refreshment stand, makes swimming and sunbathing popular too.

Let's not forget fishing. Sportsmen fish from boats as well as along the shore, and they catch fish such as bluegill, perch, walleye, catfish, bream and crappie. The largest bass caught out of Lake James weighed over fourteen pounds. Pick up some bait and rent a boat from one of the lake's landings. The Park even sponsors scheduled fishing tournaments.

The label "small town, USA" fits Marion—a regular town of average size with the usual amenities and no added frills. So after you've visited Marion's historic homes and enjoyed a little recreation at Lake James, it's time to find the falls.

Waterfalls in Bob's Creek Pocket Wilderness

3.5 mile loop, Moderate

Bob's Creek Pocket Wilderness is one of many areas set aside by the tree farming company, Bowater, for wildlife habitat, watershed protection and recreation. The primary use of Bowater's forests is to provide a base supply of timber for their two southern mills, which produce newsprint, coated paper and market pulp. Some woodlands, like Bob's Creek, have been preserved. Bowater believes in the concept of multiple-use forest management—a working forest can do more than produce timber.

Bowater purchased this particular tract from R.J. Morris in the early 1960s. With 1,067 acres, Bob's Creek is the largest of Bowater's Pocket Areas. It is considered relatively old growth for this area, probably last cut in the 1930s. You'll find an oak-hickory forest dotted with sourwood, maple, and pine. There are even a few large hemlocks.

Bowater hired a professional trail builder to do the layout. The loop is well-designed and was the first trail in North Carolina to become a National Recreation Trail. About ten minutes into the trail, there is an information board mapping out both loops. Follow the main trail signs, walking the loop clockwise (right). There are several creek crossings— some on logs and rocks, others on well-made bridges. You will pass all three waterfalls before arriving at a junction where you can choose to head back to the parking area (the 3.5 mile loop) or hike an additional 4.5 miles (a longer loop), which includes a backpacking campsite.

The waterfalls were most likely named by the trail builder, and each one is at the end of a short side trail marked with the waterfall's name. With an average height of twenty-five feet, these cascades are relatively small, but they are scenic and unique.

Hemlock Falls is surrounded, of course, by hemlock—some growing on the edge of rock cliffs. It cascades down a rock face, but one sliver of water is diverted off to the left behind a ledge, forming another tiny falls. Split Rock Falls flows through a foot-wide cut in a massive boulder and then spills over several ledges before it fans out. Hidden Falls is tucked away in a cave of rhododendron where there is barely enough room to stand up. It free-falls over an undercut lip before hitting a forty-five-degree slide where it becomes a narrow chute. Just beyond Hidden Falls, you'll find an interesting rock formation called Sentinel Rock.

As a souvenir of your hike in Bob's Creek Pocket Wilderness Area, you might want to order the "Bowater Trails" cloth patch with its forest/river design embroidered in bright blue, green, and brown. You can also can get an add-on bar that reads "Bob's Creek." To obtain these patches, write to Public Relations, Bowater, Catawba, SC 29704.

Directions: Leave Marion heading south on US 221 and go over I-40. Drive 0.5 miles past the interstate, and turn left onto Old US 221. After 1.5 miles, turn left (before Glenwood Elementary School) onto Glenwood Drive; after 0.4 miles, turn right onto Huntsville Drive. Travel 0.7 miles to the railroad tracks, another 0.4 miles to where the road becomes gravel, and then 0.2 miles to Huntsville Tower Road—turn left. After 0.6 miles, turn left again and go 1.3 miles up the mountain to the parking area at the gate. There are wooden signs directing you to Bob's Creek at several of the intersections. The trailhead is 20 feet to the left of the gate.

Tom's Creek Falls

2 mile loop, Easy

I didn't know what to expect when I visited Tom's Creek Falls. All I had was a slip of paper from the Chamber of Commerce that described it as "a gentle falls in a picturesque area." I was surprised to find a tall waterfall—one hundred feet—with sections of sheer drops ranging from five to thirty feet and a tiny pool at the base—a perfect cold-water jacuzzi for two. Car-sized boulders are scattered throughout the poplar-oak forest surrounding the falls.

The falls also has a bit of history. Two stone bridge pilings remain from a narrow-gauge railroad, which was used in the 1930s to haul out timber and transport people. More recently, the fire road, called Falls Branch Road, was built to access two small tracts cut for timber sales. Later, the forest service developed it as a strip opening—a wildlife habitat for deer, turkey, and grouse.

A note on trail directions. About 1 mile up the grassy fire road, there is an obscure trail on the left (if you pass a twenty-foot cascade on the right, you've gone too far). The trail crosses a small creek near the top of the falls and then intersects an old roadbed. Scramble down to Tom's Creek for a better view of the falls. As long as you follow the creek, you'll eventually reach Huskins Branch Road. Go left to the forest service road and return to the fire gate.

Directions: Leave Marion heading north on US 221. You will reach the community of Woodlawn after about 7 miles. Turn left on Huskins Branch Road, just before the Woodlawn Motel. Go 1.2 miles and turn right onto FS 469. There is a place to park on the left near a fire gate at 0.2 miles. The trail begins on the fire road.

Catawba Falls

3 miles roundtrip, Moderate

The trail to Catawba Falls is a popular local hike where you follow the Catawba River the whole way. I found it fascinating to watch the river change from a flat, quiet stream to a narrow, mountain creek filled with small rapids and drops. The one-hundred-foot Catawba Falls is only a few miles from the river's headwaters, which lie on the ridge to the west— the county line between McDowell and Buncombe, and the Eastern Continental Divide.

To gather more information about the falls, I phoned Mary Virginia Adams, the daughter of the original owner, Colonel Daniel W. Adams. When asked if she could answer some questions about the area, she said, "We paid taxes on that land for seventy-five years, I think I can help you."

The falls have always been open to the public. "When we owned the land, people were always welcome." The Baptist Assembly even had a permit to use the trail as part of their recreational program. Mary described Catawba Falls as a "340-foot cascade" and the upper falls as a "70-foot plunge." She suggested visiting in April after a spring rain. "The falls need rainfall because they are part of the headwaters."

To reach the falls, begin hiking on the one-hundred-year-old roadbed that runs beside a Christmas tree farm. Then ford the river on illogically placed rocks and continue upstream. Along the way, there are blackberry bushes to delight the summer visitor, and a sawmill site and old dam site that will interest the history buff.

In 1924, Colonel Adams built the old dam, as well as two powerhouses. With the help of the Catawba River, he supplied Old Fort with its first electric lights. During the last few years that the Adams family owned the land, they built the sawmill so they could sell lumber to pay the taxes on the land.

As you get close to the falls, there are unusual trail markers: bull's eyes painted in white on the rocks. Cross two feeder creeks to the right to reach the base of the falls. There is not a trail to the upper falls, but it can be reached by scrambling upstream.

In 1989, the forest service acquired 1,031 acres on the Catawba River, including the falls. It is now part of the Grandfather Ranger District of the Pisgah National Forest, and you'll see NFS boundary signs after the first quarter-mile.

Mary said the forest service is supposed to make some improvements over the next few years. She hopes the trail to the upper falls will be more accessible. And, "the tree farm would make a good parking lot."

Directions: Leave Marion heading west on I-40 to Exit 73. Drive down the ramp, take a left, and go under the interstate. Immediately turn right as if you were getting back on I-40, but at the fork, bear left instead onto Catawba River Road. The road ends after 3 miles. Pull over on the left onto the small gravel shoulder. The trail begins across the bridge and to the right. *Note:* The first quarter mile is private but there's never been a problem with access.

13

South Mountains State Park

The master plan for South Mountains State Park stresses backcountry use. In fact, of North Carolina's state parks, South Mountains has the largest emphasis on the backcountry. Relatively undeveloped, the Park retains a splendid wild quality.

The 7,400-acre park lies within a 100,000-acre region called the South Mountains. The elevations of this relatively steep terrain within the Park range from 1,250 feet along Jacob's Fork to 2,894 feet atop Benn's Knob. From the Knob, an incredible view of a string of peaks in the Blue Ridge Mountains stretches out before you.

Because the Park lies on the fall line between the piedmont and the mountains, there is a large variety of plant life. A biologist working the Park has found over eighty species of "endemic-to-endangered" plants. The Park is mostly forest—oak, pine and poplar, hickory and hemlock. This upper piedmont ecology includes laurel, rhododendron, and blueberries. Expect to find yellow birch and sycamore along the Park's streams and plenty of wildflowers in the Park's coves.

In the forest, along the streams, and in the coves, the Park houses abundant animal life. Over sixty species of birds common to the western piedmont as well as the mountains live in the Park. You might hear the black-throated green warbler or the rose-breasted grosbeak. In addition, you might see salamanders, frogs, lizards, skinks, and snakes. The white-tailed deer is prevalent, along with woodchucks, chipmunks, squirrels, raccoons and opossums.

To learn more about the Park's flora and fauna, check out the exhibits in the display cases near Jacob's Fork Picnic Area. South Mountains State Park also supports an environmental education program. Nature "walks" and ranger "talks" teach stream ecology and watershed, plants and animals, and local history. The Park schedules three wildflower hikes each year—one in the spring, the summer, and the fall.

The earliest human habitation of the South Mountains dates back to the Cherokee and the Catawba Indians. The South Mountains created a barrier between the two tribes. Archaeological data shows no proof of Indian habitation on present-day park land, but Indians must have traveled through the mountains on their way to fight. And on the summits, the Indians probably set up temporary camps for hunting and gathering food.

Permanent residents (English, Welch, Scotch-Irish, and German) began arriving in the region around 1750. Villages were established near the Catawba and French Broad Rivers. Only a few people settled in the South Mountains. Johnny Smith and his family lived on the site of the present-day park residence. Gravestones located beside the residence are the only remains of the homestead.

The South Mountains experienced a gold rush in response to an amazing discovery by wanderer Sam Martin. Local history tells the story of his visit with cobbler Bob Anderson. Martin noticed flakes of gold in the mud sealing the cracks of Anderson's log home. It was 1828, and the men headed for Brindle Creek Fork. Martin and Anderson mined forty thousand dollars worth of gold within a year.

The gold rush, which attracted thousands of prospectors, immigrants, and slave owners, lasted only a few years. The big mining companies disappeared by the late 1830s. Although a handful of locals mined into the twentieth century, no one produced more than five hundred dollars a year after 1860.

Although the first park feasibility study was completed in the early 1940s, it took thirty years of recommendations, studies, and acquisition proposals before South Mountains State Park became a reality. The North Carolina General Assembly earmarked money for state parks in 1973. Upon receiving $1.5 million, the state was able to purchase the inital 5,779 acres used to establish the Park.

In accordance with the Park's wilderness experience philosophy, South Mountains does not have a developed family campground. Camping is restricted to fourteen backpacking sites, which require registration and a small fee, and a vehicle-accessible primitive camping with eleven sites. In four locations throughout the Park, the pack-in sites require a hike of at least a mile and as much as five miles. Considered primitive camping, these grassy sites only offer fire circles, firewood, and a pit toilet. Water must be packed in.

Few state parks have a picnic facility as nice as South Mountains' main picnic area along Jacob's Fork. Streamside and dense with trees, this picnic area offers tables, grills, modern restrooms, and a display with a relief map of the Park. Another smaller picnic area requires an easy half-mile walk up to Shinny Creek. This primitive site, located in a beautiful grassy area, provides several tables and grills, a pit toilet, and additional interpretive boards.

The surface waters of South Mountains State Park consist of Jacob's Forks and its upper tributaries, Little River, and Ivy Creek, which drain into the watershed of the Catawba River. These steep, boulder-strewn creeks provide fourteen miles of trout waters, making fishing the most popular recreational activity in the Park. While most of the streams are classified wild trout waters, a two-mile section of Jacob's Fork offers fishing on delayed harvest trout waters.

In addition to fishermen, South Mountains primarily caters to hikers, mountain bikers, and horseback riders. The Park has several foot trails and bridal paths, and park roads can be used by hikers and equestrians. There are many possible loops when trails and roads are combined. If you have a mountain bike, be sure to inquire about the eighteen-mile loop around the Park.

High Shoals Falls

3 miles roundtrip, Moderate

High Shoals Falls, on Jacob's Fork, is often described as the most spectacular geologic feature in South Mountains State Park. The waterfall is spectacular but so is the extensive boardwalk that leads to the observation deck at the base of the falls.

The maze of well-designed wooden bridges allows passage across the boulder-strewn creek and up a steep ravine—over two hundred steps. At the view point, about twenty feet from the falls, you can feel the spray of Jacob's Fork as it gushes over a ledge from the top of a seventy-foot rock cliff, forming this spectacular, narrow falls.

To reach the boardwalk and the falls, take the yellow-blazed Lower Falls Trail, which begins as Headquarters Road. Signs indicate "left" at two forks, one before and one after the Shinny Creek Picnic Area. The scheduled wildflower hike in the spring, which is part of the environmental education program at South Mountains State Park, always uses this trail because of the volume and the variety of spring blooms.

In the early years of the Park, before annual visitation jumped to almost 100,000, common ravens nested in the ledges around High Shoals Falls. Like most large birds, ravens don't appreciate activity near their nests. So, they moved on. An active nest was seen as recently as 1991 at a set of cliffs in the Park called Raven Rock.

The watershed for Jacob's Fork River is extremely pure, the headwaters are contained within Park boundaries. Three major creeks, Murry Branch, Nettles Branch, and Jacob's Fork Creek, form the upper end of the river. Jacob's Fork River, one of the first rivers in North Carolina to be considered outstanding resource waters, is classified as a II ("pristine with some development") on a watershed scale from I to IV. The river contains no direct pollutants and is about as clean as surface water gets.

At the falls, the river is considered wild trout waters. A two-mile section below the junction of Jacob's Fork and Shinny Creek is considered general trout waters. This lower stretch is one of four streams in North Carolina designated "delayed harvest." This means "catch and release" during March, April, and May, and "catch and keep" during the other months of the year.

Directions: From the main parking area at South Mountains State Park, walk through Jacob's Fork Picnic Area and past the restrooms to pick up Headquarters Road.

Upper Falls

2.8 miles roundtrip, Moderate

Upper Falls is a misnomer. This statement means that Upper Falls isn't a waterfall in and of itself. High Shoals Falls actually falls a total of one hundred feet, only seventy feet can be seen from the Lower Falls Trail. The other thirty feet, labeled "Upper Falls" on old maps, cascades down a set of shoals and small pools in a picturesque area just upstream of the vertical drop of High Shoals Falls.

The trail to the top section of High Shoals Falls, called Upper Falls Trail, follows the same route to Shinny Creek Picnic Area as Lower Falls Trail. Bear right at the fork beyond the picnic grounds and ascend a gradual old roadbed. Several switchbacks climb the ridge and lead you to Upper Falls.

About a half-mile up the trail after Shinny Creek Picnic Area, there is a spring and the possible site of an old still. At one time, the area that is now South Mountains State Park, was known for its moonshine. In the Park, several torn-down stills are marked by rusted buckets and axed barrels. The name Shinny Creek was derived from the moonshining days.

For management purposes, the Park is trying to confine camping (and picnicking) to designated areas, which don't include the area around Upper Falls. The High Shoals Camping Area (pack-in sites #1-4) is to the right before you reach the river. These four wooded sites near Jacob's Fork are ideal for an easy overnighter.

An early settler to the area named Dave Bibby milled corn at the top of High Shoals Falls near the cascades of Upper Falls. He lived close to the river, and remnants—a foundation and chimney—of his homesite still remain. It is possible that Jacob's River was named after a relative of Dave Bibby named Jacob Bibby.

The Park Service is currently working on linking Lower Falls Trail and Upper Falls Trail to form a loop trail. The loop will be called High Shoals Loop Trail. They plan to construct the connecting piece—a section which will climb around the rock cliff and cross at the top of the falls—in such a way that the visitor won't see any man-made structure from the base of the waterfall.

Directions: From the main parking area at South Mountains State Park, walk Headquarters Road (see directions under High Shoals Falls) to Shinny Creek Picnic Area. A trail sign at the upper end of the picnic grounds indicates a right turn at the fork.

Little River Falls

4 miles roundtrip, Moderate

A ranger at South Mountains State Park had this to say about Little River Falls: "When it's in full water, it's every bit as pretty as High Shoals Falls." I agree! The Little River cascades down several tiers for a total of one hundred feet. Two sections each free-fall thirty to forty feet.

The trail to Little River Falls is not well developed and practically by-passes the falls. A rough footpath leads off the trail and down to the base of the waterfall. The reason? South Mountains State Park only owns the upper half of the falls just above the biggest drop. They are trying to buy the land containing the remainder of the cascade and intend to complete a trail to the bottom, as well as an observation deck and viewing area.

The land east of the trail (off to the right on the way to the falls) is South Mountain Game Land—over 4,600 acres leased to the North Carolina Wildlife Resource Commission. Little River Trail ends about one mile after the falls at Upper CCC Trail. The nearest camping to the waterfall is Little River Camping Area (pack-in sites #12-14). These three sites are located off Upper CCC Trail on Sawtooth Trail.

The watershed for the Little River is the east section of Horse Ridge where several branches come together. Part of the headwaters of the Little River is on timber land, owned by the Champion Paper Company, which was logged about fifteen years ago. A good hard rain brings silt down the mountain, so the water quality of the Little River doesn't match that of Jacob's Fork.

Directions: From the main parking area at South Mountains State Park, drive back towards the entrance for 0.4 miles to the equestrian unloading area on the left. The trailhead is directly across the road.

14

Asheville

Asheville, one of the biggest towns in the Blue Ridge, has more than 173,000 residents. The Rand McNally *Places Rated Almanac* consistently rates this city as one of the best places to live among U.S. metropolitan areas with fewer than 250,000 people. That says a lot about Asheville, but here's more.

First, because of Asheville's size, you will probably want to purchase a map. Visit Malaprop's Bookstore in the middle of downtown next to the Civic Center. In addition to purchasing a map at this local hangout, you can browse through books by area authors and sip a cappucino while listening to local music and poetry readings.

Did you know that author Thomas Wolfe spent his childhood years in Asheville at his mother's boarding house? He recreated this house in his book *Look Homeward Angel*. The Thomas Wolfe Memorial keeps up his family's Old Kentucky Home just as he would have remembered it.

You haven't been to Asheville until you've visited the Biltmore Estate. George W. Vanderbilt built his 255-room mansion in 1895, patterned after the sixteenth century chateaux of the Loire Valley in France. Famous architect Richard Morris Hunt designed the house; and landscape architect Fredrick Law Olmstead, who also designed New York's Central Park, planned the grounds.

The Biltmore House provides a visit to the elegance and opulence of Victorian society. The art work and furnishings retain their perfect condition. The extensive gardens and grounds erupt into a grand display of color in the spring. And the winery offers a look at the science and lore of wine-making.

Another of Asheville's stately mansions, the massive Grove Park Inn, stands on the opposite side of town. William Grove had the Inn built out of local stone in 1913. The lobby is eighty feet wide and almost half as long as a football field, and the mammoth fireplaces at either end burn twelve-foot logs. Like the Biltmore Estate, the feeling is one of elegance and opulence. During the summer months, horse-drawn carriages pull up in front of the Inn to take you on a tour of the town.

As the cultural center of western North Carolina, Asheville attracts artisans and craftsmen from throughout the region. Many shops display their pottery, weaving, woodworking and handmade musical instruments. The Folk Art Center, east of town at milepost 382 on the Blue Ridge Parkway, supports a retail shop as well as a gallery with outstanding exhibits. The Center holds special programs and demonstrations throughout the year. The Biltmore Village, located on US 25 before the entrance to the Biltmore Estate, was constructed to house the servants and workers who staffed the Biltmore House. Now many of the original buildings have been turned into shops. The New Morning Gallery is extremely well-known. They have a section devoted to arts and crafts that were made in North Carolina.

With its excellent restaurants, Asheville combines the variety of a big city and the quality and atmosphere of a small town. If you enjoy homemade bread and preserves, the Rollin' Pin on North Merrimon Street is a great place for breakfast. The Stone Soup downtown on Broadway features rich soups and healthy entrees—wonderful for lunch. They also have musical and story-telling events on some evenings. If you're downtown about dinnertime, try 23 Page Restaurant at Haywood Park. Breast of Chicken Old Virginia, stuffed with country ham, peanut sauce, and grits—is one of their specialties, sure to please anyone looking for a taste of the South.

Asheville hosts many convivial annual events. Every July, a downtown street festival called Bele Chere attracts more than 300,000 people for three days of music, dance, crafts, and frivolity. In August, the Mountain Dance and Folk Festival, a tradition for more than sixty years, draws bluegrass musicians and big circle square dancers to the Thomas Wolfe Auditorium in the Asheville Civic Center to compete for $2,500 in prizes. Any Saturday night in July and August, it would be worth your

Catawba rhododendrons bloom at Craggy Gardens in mid-June to early July. Photo by Frank Logue.

while to wander over to the Buncombe County Court House for Shindig-on-the-Green. This free outdoor musical event includes bluegrass, gospel and mountain music, as well as square, round, and contra (line) dancing.

But don't spend all your time in Asheville because the Blue Ridge Parkway, which passes on the east edge of town, will lead you to four waterfalls. Each waterfall is accessed from the Parkway, making the trailheads hard to miss. Just head north, watching the mile markers, and enjoy the scenery along this famous road.

Waterfalls on Carter Creek

Cascade Falls: 3.6 miles roundtrip, Moderate
Douglas Falls: 6 miles roundtrip, Strenuous
On this hike, you will discover two stands of virgin hemlock and two pretty waterfalls; of the two, the trees are the highlight of this hike. Some of the trees are eight feet around. This forest is enchanting! It doesn't take much imagination for the place to come alive with dancing fairies and tiny leprechauns.

While the trailhead is on the Blue Ridge Parkway, the majority of this white-blazed path is in the Big Ivy Area of Pisgah National Forest. The forest service did not do maintenance work on the Falls Trail in 1992 or 1993 because the park service may relocate their section. For the most accurate information and directions, be sure to check with the visitor center at the trailhead where you'll also find exhibits and a small store.

The trailhead is in Craggy Gardens, a Blue Ridge Parkway recreation area that is famous for its balds. Balds aren't completely bare: grassy balds support wildflowers, grasses, and other low-growing plants, and heath balds support shrubs like rhododendron, laurel and flame azalea. Scientists don't agree on why these balds exist. Some believe man cleared the land for livestock or to attract game, others blame fire or drastic climate change.

Don't miss seeing the balds between mid-June and early July when the pink and purple blooms of the native rhododendron star in the most dazzling flower pageant on the Parkway. These shrubs color the slopes and peaks of the Craggies, acre after acre.

In addition to the balds and rhododendron display, Craggy Gardens has gnarled trees. The beech, birch and mountain ash have been twisted and dwarfed by the severe wind/ice storms and the short growing season at this elevation (5,500 feet).

Directions: Pick up the Blue Ridge Parkway in Asheville by first heading east on I-240 and exiting onto US 74. After about 0.5 miles on US 74, you will drive under the Parkway. Take a right and go up the ramp to access the Parkway. You will be near milepost 385. (Several signs along the route direct you to the Blue Ridge Park-way.) Travel north for about 20 miles. Craggy Gardens Visitor Center is at milepost 364.6. The trailhead is at the upper end of the north parking area.

Mitchell Falls

Not accessible

Mitchell Falls lies on private land just outside the western boundary of Mt. Mitchell State Park. Even though the falls are not accessible to the public, there is a story worth telling. The forty-foot Mitchell Falls was named for Elisha Mitchell, a native of Connecticut and professor at the University of North Carolina. Mitchell fell to his death from the falls while trying to prove his claim that Mt. Mitchell was the highest peak in the East.

In June 1857, he was re-measuring the mountain because his earlier findings had been challenged. A search party led by Big Tom Wilson, a local backwoodsman, found his body in a deep pool below the falls. Elisha Mitchell is buried on his mountain near the observation tower.

Mt. Mitchell, combined with eighteen peaks over 6,300 feet, form the highest range in the East, the Black Mountains. They were named for the dark green color of the spruce and fir trees. For more than a billion years, wind and water rounded the towering pinnacles; the resistant igneous and metamorphic rock of Mt. Mitchell endured.

In 1916, as a result of Governor Craig's efforts, the area became North Carolina's first state park. The second highest peak in the East, Mount Craig (6,647 feet), was named in his honor. Besides the most impressive view around, this 1,677-acre park has tent camping, picnic grounds, a restaurant and a small weather station. The Park has a bookstore at the interpretive center and several good hiking trails.

The museum, my favorite place in Mt. Mitchell State Park, allowed me to meet Elisha. Half the building is dedicated to sharing his story. There are photographs of Elisha, Big Tom and Mitchell Falls. You will even find the last letter Elisha wrote to his wife before his death.

When you visit the Park, it's hard not to notice the dying trees. The two dominate species, Fraser fir (found above 5,500 feet) and red spruce (found as low as 4,500 feet), are disappearing. In the last ten years, the death rate of virgin timber has been startling. Scientists believe there are several contributing factors, including harmful insects and high ozone levels. Extreme weather—winds of one hundred miles per hour, ice storms and a growing season of only four months—also plays a big role.

Directions: Although this waterfall is not accessible, you can visit Mt. Mitchell State Park. Pick up the Parkway in Asheville (see directions under Waterfalls on Carter Creek) and head north for about 30 miles.

Turn left onto NC 128 at milepost 355.4 and travel 5 miles to the parking area near the summit. The Park is closed on Christmas Day and during periods of heavy snow.

Glassmine Falls

No hike necessary

From a Parkway pull-off (at 5,197 feet), you can look across the valley and see Glassmine Falls sliding 800 feet down Horse Range Ridge. Surprised? It is hard to judge height when a waterfall is so far away.

Glassmine Falls is part of the Asheville Watershed. Rivers and creeks run down the slopes of this valley into the North Fork Reservoir, and the water is pumped to the city. So Glassmine Falls plays a part in supplying water to the people in Asheville.

Near the base of the falls, from an old pit mine and cabin site, miners hauled out mica on pack animals and carried it to the Toe River Valley—Micaville and Burnsville—in the early 1900s. It is the oldest mineral industry in the area, and a truckload of high-quality mica could bring in thousands of dollars then. Mica used to be referred to as isinglass, and people in the mountains called it "glass." The waterfall got its name from the "glass mine."

This is a wet-weather falls, which means it will almost disappear during periods of low water. If you can't visit Glassmine Falls after a heavy rain, try late afternoon. With the sun shining on the falls, the wet rock face looks like glass.

An observation area with a wooden bench—up the paved sidewalk and to the left—makes a nice rest stop. In addition to the view east of Glassmine Falls, look west for an incredible view of Roan Mountain. Binoculars and a camera lens with a focal length of at least 200mm will make this waterfall more fun.

Directions: Pick up the Parkway in Asheville (see directions under Waterfalls on Carter Creek) and head north for about 25 miles. Turn into the overlook for Glassmine Falls on the right at milepost 361.2.

15

Transylvania County

Transylvania County, long touted as "The Land of the Water falls," boasts of literally hundreds of falls, cascades, shoots, slides, and showers—every type of falling water imaginable. The falls in this area can occupy devoted waterfall hikers for weeks. Transylvania County quite possibly has more waterfalls than any other county in the United States.

The area's sizeable number of waterfalls is due to the county's great variance in elevation and hundreds of miles of streams. From 6,025 feet on top of Chestnut Bald in the northwest, the terrain drops to 1,100 feet where the Toxaway River meets Lake Jocassee at the border of South Carolina.

The French Broad, the major river in Transylvania County, flows through the Sylvan Valley to the county's eastern border. Many prominent streams empty into the French Broad within the county, including the Davidson and Little Rivers, and Catheys and Carson Creeks. The Whitewater, Thompson, Horsepasture, and Toxaway Rivers are at the southern end of the county. Other significant waterways in the south are Indian Creek, Bear Wallow Creek, Toxaway Creek, and Rock Creek. All of these spill into Duke Power Company's Lake Jocassee.

Hundreds of other arterial streams flow throughout the county. Many of the creeks have multiple waterfalls. The North Fork of the French Broad River alone has twenty, and the West Fork has nineteen. Bear Wallow Creek sports ten waterfalls.

Jim Bob Tinsley, Transylvania County's foremost authority on waterfalls, wrote *Land of the Waterfalls*, the definitive volume on waterfalls in the area and a fascinating account of the stories behind the waterfalls. Trained as an aerial photographer in the U.S. Navy during World War II, Jim Bob has chronicled the background of the Transylvania waterfalls through his photographs and captivating tales. Some of the mills and other structures in his photographs no longer exist except through these photographs.

Having grown up in Transylvania County, this retired educator knows more about the history and topography of the area than anyone you will meet. Along with being an accomplished author, Jim Bob is a cowboy singer of great renown. Jim Bob's many achievements will soon be honored in the Jim Bob Tinsley Museum in Brevard.

We had the great fortune to spend a day of waterfall hiking with Jim Bob and his wife, Dottie, as our guides. And what an adventure it was! Many of the "trails" Jim Bob led us on had been overgrown for years. We crossed over creeks, under barbed wire, and through dense laurel thickets with Jim Bob in the lead and Dottie matching him step-for-step. At Frozen Creek Falls, our expert guide pointed to the remnants of a once flourishing grist mill. Jim Bob photographed this, and many other area mills, in the 1950s.

Because of his knowledge of waterfalls and area history, Jim Bob teaches a popular adult education course on the subject at Brevard College. His well-recognized expertise as a photographer and historian fills the class up quickly. During the three-day course, he leads his students to as many as twenty waterfalls.

Jim Bob Tinsley's fascination with waterfalls began when he was a very young boy. Having grown up in the "Land of the Waterfalls," Jim Bob says that waterfalls have been an important part of his life. For us, having discovered the joy of these falling wonders in recent years, it was indeed a privilege to have seen some of them through the eyes of "Mr. Waterfall."

Because of the incredible number of waterfalls in Transylvania County, we have divided the area into three base towns—Brevard, Pisgah Forest, and Lake Toxaway. Brevard, the county seat, sits near the center

Moore Cove Falls in Pisgah National Forest is one of hundreds of waterfalls in Transylvania County that gave the county the reputation as the"Land of the Waterfalls." Photo by Ben Keys.

of the county. To the east, the quiet crossroads of the community of Pisgah Forest opens the door to the Pisgah District of Pisgah National Forest. The southwest corner of the county hosts the quaint resort town of Lake Toxaway.

Look on the next page and begin reading about the area history and attractions of Brevard, Pisgah Forest, and Lake Toxaway. In the next three chapters, details on various waterfalls in the "Land of the Waterfalls" follows each base town.

16

Brevard

Brevard, the county seat of Transylvania County, once belonged to the Indians, as did most of Appalachia. Before white traders began coming from South Carolina and parts of North Carolina, numerous Indian paths criss-crossed present-day Brevard. The first white settlers were enticed here in the middle of the eighteenth century, by the rich soil and abundant game. They called it "Cherokee Crossing" and referred to the clearings in the forests that the Indians burned to make hunting easier as "mountain prairies."

The territory that became Transylvania County was not made available for grants until after 1785, when a treaty with the Cherokee transferred the land to the government. Revolutionary soldiers received some of the grants for their service to the colony. According to George H. Smathers's book *The History of Land Titles in Western North Carolina*, one of the first land grants—fifty acres on Catheys Creek, about four miles west of Brevard—was given to William Porter on October 11, 1783.

On February 15, 1861, a government act provided for the formation of Transylvania County from Henderson and Jackson Counties. The first court session, held at the "Valley Store" of B.C. Lankford on May 20, 1861, established a committee of citizens to select a permanent seat of justice to be named Brevard and to be located within five miles of William Probart Poor's store. (The "Valley Store" was later the location of Straus Elementary School, and Poor's store was located on the site of the present-day Red House.) The court also authorized paying volunteer soldiers the sum of fifteen dollars. This timely decision occurred on the same day that North Carolina voted to secede from the Union. The newly formed Transylvania County found itself at war.

The county seat of Brevard was incorporated in 1868 and named in honor of Dr. Ephraim Brevard. Unfortunately, the prominent surgeon and Revolutionary Colonel never laid eyes on the town which bears his name. Famous for having penned the Mecklenberg Declaration of Independence in 1775, which did not surface until long after Thomas Jefferson's Declaration in 1776, Dr. Brevard helped establish Queens College in Charlotte, North Carolina. He practiced medicine and taught at the college. During the Revolution, the British captured Colonel Brevard in Charleston, where he died in prison of an unknown disease at the age of thirty-seven.

In 1985, the citizens of Brevard erected a statue in Ephraim Brevard's honor in front of the city offices on West Main Street. While many proclaim him "Father of the City," others say that the town was named for all the Brevard brothers. There were seven, all heroes of the Revolution.

Like all pioneer communities, especially mountainous ones, the little town of Brevard suffered the economic calamity of isolation. The few roads that existed were little more than ruts. And the one vainglorious attempt to navigate a steamship on the shallow and swiftly flowing French Broad River ended in disaster.

In 1876, Colonel S.V. Pickens formed the French Broad Steamboat Company. Under the colonel's leadership, the company built "The Mountain Lily," a sidewheel steamer capable of carrying almost one hundred passengers. After completing ship, the company determined that the river was too shallow. Workers hauled in huge loads of rocks in an attempt to alter the river's flow and make the channel deeper. The day of the launch arrived amid much fanfare and ballyhoo. The excitement reached such a pitch, Brevard declared a holiday.

The accounts of what actually happened that day vary. (1) A sudden downpour caused the Mountain Lily to become stranded on a sandbar before she ever made the trip. (2) The steamboat didn't clear a low bridge that her builders had not taken into consideration. (3) The ship made the roundtrip from Mud Creek to Elmbend Bridge before sinking at the dock. Whatever happened, the Mountain Lily's maiden voyage was also her last.

Mud that jammed the jetties interfered with the river's natural flow. To add insult to injury, the taxpayers lost forty-three thousand dollars. The only tangible reminder of the Mountain Lily is Horseshoe Baptist Church, which was built with lumber from the ship and her bell was mounted in the steeple. Luckily for Transylvania County, the railroad was on its way.

In 1894, the first train came to Brevard on the Hendersonville and Brevard Railroad. By 1899, two trains ran daily between these two mountain towns. The railroad marked the beginning of an unprecedented boom for the county.

Railroads always attracted men of wealth and power. It was no different for Brevard. Industrialists who came to the area from Pennsylvania with great visions of a glorious future encouraged development of the county. These men, instrumental in Brevard's economic development, included Joseph S. Silversteen, who arrived in 1859, and J. Frances Hayes, who arrived in 1890.

A civic and community leader, Joseph S. Silversteen bought 140 thousand acres of forest land and set up lumber mills at Rosman, just southwest of Brevard. Among Silversteen's other ventures were the Toxaway Tanning Company, founded in 1901, and the Gloucester Lumber Company, founded in 1911.

Silvermont, Silversteen's legacy to Brevard, is a colonial revival mansion built in 1917 on eight acres of East Main Street near the business district. The Friends of Silvermont formed in 1981 to maintain the estate, which is on the National Register of Historic Places. Today, the mansion hosts meetings and special functions.

J.F. Hayes supposedly came south for health reasons, but as an entrepreneur, he must have also been attracted by the lumber and other natural resources. In 1896, Hayes organized the Toxaway Company, which was responsible for building Brevard's first fine hotel, the Franklin, in 1900. Visitors enjoyed luxurious accommodations and a "real bath." The Franklin was just the beginning for Hayes, who went on to build many other resorts that catered to wealthy tourists.

Today, Brevard offers small-town charm and a genteel hospitality—just the sort of place most of us would like to settle. In addition to the area's bountiful natural resources, Brevard has fine music, an outstanding theater, and several arts festivals.

The Brevard Chamber Orchestra, organized in 1976, presents three concerts each year. The group includes many notable musicians from western North Carolina and also presents guest artists. Long known as "The Summer Music Center of the South," the town is also home to the Brevard Music Center, recognized as one of the five major institutions of its type in the country. Each summer students come here from all over the world to study and perform with faculty and guest artists on the 120-acre campus located in the Blue Ridge Mountains on the outskirts of Brevard. Founded in 1936 by Dr. James C. Pfohl at Davidson College, the Center moved to its present location in 1944.

The forty-three-year-old Brevard Little Theater, an active local theater company, does several productions each year. Annually, the "Festival of the Arts" runs during the second week of July, featuring art shows, craft exhibits and demonstrations, and musical events.

Brevard College, a two-year institution, occupies 140 beautiful acres near the center of town. Three schools merged in 1934 to form Brevard College: Rutherford College (chartered 1853), Weaver College (chartered 1872), and Brevard Institute (chartered 1895). The majority of Brevard College graduates go on to four-year schools.

Brevard offers great shopping—antiques, collectibles, and crafts. The White Squirrel Shoppe and the Workshop & Company at Jordan Street Center sell antiques, unique white squirrel memorabilia, local crafts, and handcrafted furniture. If you appreciate pottery, don't miss Mud Dabber's Pottery and Crafts, located four miles south of town on Greenville Highway (US 276). Run by the John Dodson family, the unique handcrafted creations are irresistible.

A number of charming bed and breakfast establishments in the area include The Red House on West Probart Street and The Womble Inn on Main Street. Built in 1851, The Red House was Brevard's first post office as well as William Poor's store. The structure has been renovated and added to over the years, but the foundation is considered to be the oldest in town.

The Womble Inn has a homey atmosphere and rooms furnished with 18th and 19th century antiques. The innkeepers, Beth and Steve Womble, act as gracious hosts. If you would like to take a picnic on one of your waterfall hikes, Beth provides a delectable specialty food basket from her "Repasts" at The Womble Inn.

Across the street from The Womble Inn, Oh! Susanna's serves up fresh food, a laid-back atmosphere, and friendly service. We especially enjoyed the Christmas tree that adorned the dining room when we were there in February.

The snow-white squirrels that can be seen in Brevard's Franklin Park off Franklin Street and in some of the wooded neighborhoods are not albinos. These rare species trace their roots back to a pair brought in 1949 by H.H. Mull as a gift to his niece. One account says he bought the squirrels from a ship's captain in Florida, another version says he obtained them after they escaped from an overturned carnival truck. At any rate, inevitably one of the squirrels escaped, so the family let the other one go, hoping they would find one another. They did, and today an estimated two hundred white squirrels scamper around Brevard.

You can learn more about Brevard through a photographic exhibit at the Transylvania County Courthouse on the corner of Broadway and East Main. Completed in 1861 and registered as a National Historic Place, the courthouse features a square central Italianate-style tower. The Brevard/Transylvania County Chamber of Commerce, under the direction of Esther Wesley, also provides excellent information.

It is easy to see why Rand McNally recommends Brevard as an ideal retirement spot. Spend some time exploring this delightful mountain community. But ultimately, we hope that your adventures will lead you to the rivers and waterways that are hosts to the sparkling, tumbling waters for which this area is so well-known.

Key Falls

0.4 miles roundtrip, Easy

Would you like to take a step back in time? On the grounds of the Key Falls Inn, a small but charming cascade quietly invites you to linger at this quaint country inn and take in the peaceful vista of the tranquil valleys of the French Broad and Davidson Rivers. A magnificent view includes the distant Mt. Pisgah.

A short trail begins at the inn and takes you to the top of the falls, where a small wooden bridge spans the spring-fed creek. With water rushing just inches below, you overlook the stream, winding its way to the French Broad River, which borders the property. Surrounded by the melody of rippling water, you can watch the sun set behind the Pisgah Ridge Mountains.

Key Falls is a low-volume falls, but its modest supply of water is amplified by some thirty-eight stair-step ledges. This results in the hundreds of small cascades that form the eighty-foot waterfall. The creek runs under the road and feeds the picturesque pond beside the Key Falls Inn. The pond has two docks for fishing or just sitting and taking in this enchanting scene.

Key Falls is part of thirty-five acres surrounding the Key Falls Inn. The quaint bed and breakfast establishment was once the home of Charles Patton, one of the committeemen who laid out the town of Brevard in 1861. Constructed of wood, sand, and rock from the nearby mountainside, the home was started in 1860 but was not finished until after the Civil War in 1868. While the site was not involved in any battles, the open field beside the inn is believed to have served as an encampment for confederate soldiers.

The large Victorian farmhouse was opened as a bed and breakfast in 1989. It is the perfect place to rest tired muscles after a full day of waterfall hiking. Nestled in a peaceful valley, it is hard to imagine a more ideal setting for a country inn. The gracious owners offer genuine hospitality, making guests feel like part of the family. If you leave hungry after one of Patricia Grosvenor's delicious breakfasts, you have only yourself to blame.

Directions: From the Chamber of Commerce building (35 West Main Street) in downtown Brevard, go left on North Broad (East US 64) for 0.9 miles. Make a right on Old H-Ville Highway (Old US 64) and follow it for 2.7 miles. Go right on Everett Road for 0.4 miles and then right again on Seven Springs Road just past the entrance to the Key Falls Inn. The falls are on the left, 0.2 miles up the hill. Park at the base of the falls. The trailhead is 100 yards back down the road on the right. (Although Key Falls is on private land, the owners at the Key Falls Inn are glad to share this beautiful waterfall with the public.)

Connestee Falls

0.4 miles roundtrip, Moderate

Connestee Falls is often referred to as a double falls. Actually, it is a three-tiered falls that is joined at its base by Batson Creek Falls, a separate waterfall that enhances the appeal of a hike to Connestee Falls. The two cascades are viewed together from a well-maintained trail that leads to the bottom of Connestee Falls.

Emanating from Lake Atagahi, Carson Creek pours a hefty sixteen thousand gallons a minute over three rock ledges that form Connestee Falls. The modest Carson Creek broadens into a twenty-five foot wide drape of roaring water as it drops over the first and most precipitous ledge. The waters plunge a total of 110 feet before merging with the output from Batson Creek.

Originating from Lake Ticoa, Batson Creek emerges from the south to glide over a granite dome and also drop 110 feet, creating Batson Creek Falls. Batson Creek Falls has less volume than Connestee Falls. However, when the creeks converge and are squeezed between two rock walls, the result is a wild sluice of water know as Silver Slip. The consolidated waters journey north and eventually join the French Broad River.

Carson Creek was named after Revolutionary War veteran, John Carson. He began his military career fighting the Cherokee Indians until a greater enemy came along, the South Carolina Tories. In 1795, after the war for independence was won, Carson moved to Transylvania

Connestee Falls once had a grist mill at the head of the falls. Photo by Ben Keys.

County and acquired a large parcel of land adjacent to the creek that bears his name.

The land changed hands many times during the ensuing years. William Probart Poor, Brevard's prominent judge, once paid five dollars for one hundred acres on Carson Creek which included an "unknown shoal." This shoal later became known as Connestee Falls. Probart Street in Brevard was once named Poor Street in honor of Judge Poor. Due to local objection, the name was changed to the judge's middle name. It seems no one liked the idea of living on "Poor" Street.

In 1870, a grist mill was constructed at the lip of the falls. An old photo hanging in the Connestee Falls Realty Office shows the mill perched upon the ledge over-looking Connestee Falls.

Connestee Falls got its name from a beautiful Cherokee Indian princess who jumped to her death after her white husband was lured back to live among his people. It has been rumored that her broken-hearted spirit still roams the scene of her demise. On moonlit nights at the place where the two waterfalls become one, you would not be the first to catch a glimpse of the woeful Princess Connestee.

Connestee Falls is privately owned and maintained. Until recently, viewing the falls was not a problem. Unfortunately, Connestee Falls is up for sale and presently closed to the public.

Directions: From the Chamber of Commerce building (35 West Main Street) in downtown Brevard, go one half block and take US 276 south for 6 miles to Connestee Falls. There is a large parking lot serving both the Connestee Falls Realty Office and the trail to the falls.

Raven Cliff Falls

4.4 miles roundtrip, Strenuous

Matthews Creek pours over the top of Raven Cliff and plunges four hundred feet to the valley that lies between Coldbranch Mountain and Caesar's Head Mountain. South Carolina's most breathtaking waterfall, Raven Cliff Falls is a combination of sheer drops, rushing torrents, lazy pools, sliding fans, and racing cascades. Mathews Creek then joins the Middle Saluda as it carves its way through the valley called "the dismal," named for the stifling heat.

The creek begins with a thirty-foot free-fall into a pool, and then rushes around both sides of a huge boulder to form two long cascades. This is followed by an eighty-foot drop onto a massive granite shelf, a forty-foot sliding fan, and several more cascades and smaller falls.

For those who enjoy a hearty hike, getting to Raven Cliff Falls is half the fun. The trail alternates between modest inclines, level ground, and steep descents as you hike through the undulating topography. After approximately three-quarters of a mile, you reach a ridge buffeted by a strong wind. At an altitude of over thirty-two hundred feet, you have a one-hundred-mile view of the Piedmont plain below—called the Blue Ridge escarpment. From here you can see Parris Mountain, Blue Rock, and Table Rock beyond the Greenville Watershed.

The path then drops through a rhododendron thicket, complete with the sounds of a rushing creek. After several descending switchbacks, the trail ends at an observation deck. The falls are viewed across a wide open valley. Although you are approximately one-half mile from the falls, binoculars are not necessary to enjoy the panoramic scene.

Raven Cliff Falls and the surrounding acreage was owned and preserved by the Moore and Mills families of South Carolina. It was donated to the state in 1981 and is now part of the Caesar's Head State Park. The predominant feature of the Park and one of South Carolina's most famous landmarks is Caesar's Head, a massive granite formation which some think resembles the head of Julius Caesar. Although this sounds like a reasonable explanation for the derivation of the name, there are those that believe the famous cliff obtained its name from the Indian word for chieftain, "sachem." Whatever the origin, Caesar's Head State Park offers hiking, camping, a well-maintained trail system, and a magnificent view from Caesar's Head Lookout.

Directions: From the Chamber of Commerce building (35 West Main Street) in downtown Brevard, take US 276 for 14.1 miles (8 miles past Connestee Falls) south to Raven Cliff Falls in South Carolina. The parking area is reached shortly after crossing the state line, but it is easy to miss because the only sign is not readily visible for motorists traveling south from Brevard. Cars parked along the roadway will indicate the correct location. The well-marked trailhead is on the right side of the road opposite the parking area.

17

Pisgah Forest

Transylvania means "across the woods." Most of Transylvania County's 250,000 acres are forested, so the translation is a fitting one. The community of Pisgah Forest exists because of these woodlands. The town is centered around the Carr Lumber Company, which in the early part of this century purchased a thirty-year contract for timber rights to forest property on George Vanderbilt's Biltmore Estate. This land became the nucleus of the Pisgah National Forest. Today, trains still travel to and from the community of Pisgah Forest, carrying freight for the Carr Lumber Company.

About eighty-three thousand acres of Transylvania County is national forest. Established in 1916, Pisgah National Forest is the oldest national forest in the East. The vast woodland of Nantahala and Pisgah National Forests cover over one million acres in parts of twelve North Carolina counties, making it the state's largest public natural resource.

Pisgah was the Biblical mountain from which Moses first looked upon the Promised Land (Deuteronomy 34:1). This verdant wonderland held great "promise" for George Vanderbilt, the visionary who saw its potential.

In the late 1800s, Vanderbilt began acquiring land in the area around Asheville for his fabulous Biltmore Estate, fashioned after a 16th century French chateau. He purchased farms and estates, eventually buying more than 125,000 acres. These vast holdings consisted of lush mountain timberland, including Mt. Pisgah, a 5,721-foot peak.

Vanderbilt initially hired conservationist Gifford Pinchot to manage his forests and game preserve. Pinchot (who later became governor of Pennsylvania and first Chief of the U.S. Forest Service) planned and oversaw the renovation of Vanderbilt's forest, much of which was badly eroded. His was the first comprehensive forest management system in the Western Hemisphere.

Pinchot's success with the Biltmore timberland encouraged Vanderbilt to purchase additional acreage around Mt. Pisgah. Many of the primary ideas of American forestry began and developed in the forests of the Biltmore Estate. Pinchot was influential in the establishment of the United States Forest Service in 1905.

Pinchot's successor at Biltmore was the famous German forest meister, Carl A. Schenck. Known as the "Father of American Forestry," Dr. Schenck established this country's first school of forestry in 1898 at the Biltmore Estate. Under Vanderbilt's sponsorship, Schenck was prompted to start the school to answer the questions of his inquisitive apprentices. The school met at the Biltmore Estate in the winter months, while summer sessions were held in Pisgah Forest. With the onset of World War I, the last class of the Biltmore Forest School graduated and supplied the United States with many of its early foresters.

After George Vanderbilt's death in 1914, much of his forest land was deeded to or purchased by the government. Thus, Biltmore Estate property became one of the first tracts of the Pisgah National Forest. Some of the original Biltmore Estate land was also allocated to the Blue Ridge Parkway.

Pisgah National Forest is comprised of the Pisgah, Toecane, French Broad, and Grandfather Districts. The Pisgah District (156,103 acres) is the flagship of all of North Carolina's national forest districts, and one of the most visited. In this district alone, there are over 400 miles of trails and several outstanding attractions and historic firsts.

In 1968, Congress passed the Cradle of Forestry in America Act, which set aside sixty-four thousand acres within the Pisgah National Forest to commemorate the birthplace of Carl Schenck's Biltmore Forest School. The Act designated the school as a National Natural Historic Site. Named the Cradle of Forestry in America, the school has been restored and reconstructed to offer visitors a fine exhibit of the history of the first scientific forestry practiced in America.

The exhibit consists of two interpretive trails off US 276. The Biltmore Forest Campus Trail is a 0.9 mile loop that takes the visitor past original as well as reconstructed buildings of the forest school. The "campus" consisted of mountain cabins and farm homes that were part of an area know historically as the "Pink Beds" community. The Black Forest lodges, which were used to house the rangers, were replicas of those built in Germany's Black Forest.

There was also a blacksmith shop, a commissary, and the one-room community schoolhouse, which served as the classroom. The school-house was also the church, were Schenck was known to preach from time to time. He even donated an organ hoping, he said, to "improve the singing." Alumni of the Biltmore Forest School funded the reconstruction of the school in 1966.

In 1908, the Biltmore Forest Fair was organized to demonstrate the work being done at the school. The one-mile Forest Festival Trail in the Pisgah District features exhibits similar to those seen at the fair, including a 1900 steam-powered sawmill and a 1915 climax logging locomotive.

Near the Cradle of Forestry, the Pink Beds adorn a mountain valley at 3,250 feet below Pisgah Ledge. The "pink" is in reference to the pink phlox, laurel, rhododendron, and wild azaleas (known locally as mountain honeysuckle) that cover the highland area in late spring and early summer. The scenic spot has wonderful picnic facilities.

One of the most visited spots in the Pisgah District is Sliding Rock Falls, where Dr. Schenck's forestry students once enjoyed a breakneck ride down what has been called "the fastest sixty feet in the mountains." At Sliding Rock, the waters of Looking Glass Creek flow at eleven thousand gallons per minute over an eel-slick rock formation, plummeting the intrepid adventurer into an icy, seven-foot pool. The spot was once known as Slick Rock by locals, who enjoyed having it to themselves. Now they must share this popular attraction with the thousands of tourists who come here every year. This is a great people-watching spot; even if you're not bold enough to take the plunge yourself, you'll enjoy watching those who do.

Another rock, whose presence dominates the Pisgah District is Looking Glass Rock. This seventeen-hundred-foot granite monolith watches over the woods like a giant sentinel, never sleeping. The Cherokee called it "the devil's looking glass" because of the way the winter sunlight reflected off the frozen side of the mountain.

The Pisgah District lies within the annual migratory path of the Monarch butterflies, their path crossing the Blue Ridge Parkway between the Looking Glass Rock Parking Area (milepost 417) and Wagon Road Gap (milepost 411). These stunning orange and black insects are the only butterflies that migrate on a regular basis. In September, they fly south to Mexico, where they breed in the spring. Their offspring return to the starting point, usually somewhere in New York, Pennsylvania, or Ontario.

One of the largest fish hatcheries in the East is located in the Pisgah District. Operated by the North Carolina Wildlife Resources Commission, the hatchery, located on the Davidson River, raises thousands of trout each year. They are used to stock the streams of the forest from March through August. The hatchery raises brook (speckled), brown, and rainbow trout, as well as an unusual golden trout that was developed here.

The Bent Creek Experimental Forest on the north edge of the Pisgah District is home to a number of state champion trees. Part of the original Biltmore Estate acreage, it was designated by the U.S. Forest Service for research on the regeneration of southern hardwoods.

Information on all of the Pisgah District attractions can be obtained at the ranger station just inside the district on US 276. Brochures, maps, and trail information are available. The rangers are friendly and helpful. Winter hours are from 8:00 A.M. until 4:30 P.M., Monday through Friday. The station is open on weekends from April through October.

Gifford Pinchot's philosophy was that national forests exist because the people want them. Because of men such as Pinchot, Carl Schenck, and George Vanderbilt, these forests have been preserved. The waterfalls of the Pisgah District of the Pisgah National Forest are among its most enticing and beautiful features. Some of the falls are easily accessible, while others require a bit more time and effort to reach. Whatever level of adventure you seek, you're sure to enjoy the waterfalls around Pisgah Forest.

Mill Shoals Falls

No hike necessary

Within the Balsam Grove Area of Pisgah National Forest, two watersheds converge behind the Living Waters Ministries Center to form a double waterfall known as Mill Shoals Falls. The North Fork of the French Broad River flows from the northwest and tumbles ten feet over a river-wide rock shelf, creating a sixty-foot curtain of water; and Shoal Creek joins the French Broad from the northeast a short distance downstream.

Mill Shoals Falls is among the easiest and most accessible falls in the area. Plus, you drive right past them on the way to Courthouse Falls. Just leave the parking area and walk to the left and behind the house.

You can stand on one the many rocks at the base of the falls to view the 180-degree panorama of falling water. The roar of the water from this waterfall drowns out all sounds from the nearby road, giving the impression of being in the middle of the wilderness.

Mill Shoals is mistakenly referred to as Bird Rock Falls by locals and tourist literature. Bird Rock Falls is actually 0.25 miles downstream and gets its name from the one-hundred-foot-high granite cliff that served the nesting needs for hundreds of purple martins. Over the years, Mill Shoals has been called by many other names, such as French Broad Falls and Twin Falls. It also earned the name Elysium Falls, which means "a place of happiness." Whatever the name, we call it beautiful!

Directions: From the Pisgah Ranger Station in Pisgah Forest, travel south on US 276 for 1.4 miles to US 64. Head west on US 64 for 12 miles past Brevard, to Rosman. Turn right onto NC 215 and drive north for 7.7 miles. The Living Waters Ministries will be on the left. There is a parking lot, but because the waterfall is on private land, ask permission before viewing.

Mill Shoals Falls has also been known as French Broad Falls and Twin Falls. Photo by Ben Keys.

Courthouse Falls

0.6 miles roundtrip, Easy

Courthouse Falls is also called Coon Dog Falls. While on the hunt, a hound was swept away by the current and inadvertently took the plunge. Unbelievably, this cataract was successfully descended recently by daredevil kayakers who, like the lucky hound, lived to bark about it.

Flowing through the Balsam Grove Area of Pisgah National Forest, Courthouse Creek is a major tributary of the North Fork of the French Broad River. Courthouse Creek charges through Summey Cove picking up speed as the gradient increases.

The forceful water drops over a series of five-foot ledges before reaching the precipice, where it is squeezed between rock outcroppings and its power is released down a vertical rock face. The result is the magnificent, fifty-foot Courthouse Falls. The last ten feet free-falls into a cauldron of bubbling, dark green water. The granite walls at the fall's base have been eroded by the circular flow of the current, creating an interesting whirlpool effect.

The Summey Cove Trail leads to Courthouse Creek Falls. It follows the creek along an abandoned railroad bed left over from World War I logging days. While you could go on walking along this level trail for several miles, you want to take a left at the trail marker for the falls. This will lead you down a switchback and then a staircase to the base of the falls.

Courthouse Creek originates around Devil's Courthouse Mountain, which also houses the headwaters of the Wild and Scenic Chattooga River. Cherokee Indian legend tells of a giant slant-eyed devil named Judaculla who resided deep inside the mountain. Within his dark legal chambers, Judaculla passed final judgment on departing souls. This gateway to the spirit world was held in reverence by the Cherokee people, and the waters that emerged were considered sacred.

Directions: From the Pisgah Ranger Station in Pisgah Forest, travel south on US 276 for 1.4 miles to US 64. Head west on US 64 for 12 miles past Brevard, to Rosman. Turn right onto NC 215 and drive north for 10 miles. Turn right on FS 140 (Courthouse Creek Road). Follow this gravel road for 3 miles. Immediately after the fourth bridge, park in the small pull-off on the right. The Summey Cove trailhead is across the road to the right of Courthouse Creek.

Twin Falls

3.8 miles roundtrip, Easy

Everyone likes those "buy one, get one free" specials at the grocery store because you get double the goods for the same price. This is also true for Twin Falls. On this hike, you get two distinct waterfalls for your efforts; and like fraternal twins, each waterfall has its own special characteristics.

The first waterfall, fed by springs from Rich Mountain, is an eighty-foot cascade. The trail crosses at the waterfalls' base, giving you an excellent view as the moderate volume leaps over the edge high above. While the water splashes its way down rock ledges, there are rocks in the creek at the base that allow you to stay dry if you are photographing the scene.

The second waterfall is just thirty yards from the first. The low volume drift from this fall is light and airy, trailing down seventy-five feet like a bride's veil. The water collects at the base to form a small rivulet, which joins its twin's creek a short distance down the valley. The creek flows adjacent to the Buckhorn Gap Trail, eventually merging with Avery Creek.

Although these falls are becoming increasingly popular, you will most likely be alone on this walk because these falls do not appear on the trail maps available at the ranger station. Follow the blue blazes, then the yellow blazes of Avery Creek Trail for 0.9 miles. This is also a horse trail so be sure to follow the footpath signs. Take the orange-blazed Buckhorn Gap Trail for 0.6 miles to the Twin Falls Loop Trail, which is blue blazed and circles around in either direction for 0.4 miles to both falls.

We keep our young children interested on long hikes by playing a game we call "Keeper of the Bridge." When we come to a bridge, the "Keeper" blocks the path and won't allow passage until each person solves a riddle. If you play the game on this trail, have some riddles handy because there are nine stream crossings, seven with log bridges. (If you're not adept at solving riddles, this could be a three-day hike!)

Directions: From the Pisgah Ranger Station in Pisgah Forest, travel 0.6 miles north on US 276, turn right on FS 477, and follow this gravel road for 2.5 miles. At 1.7 miles, you will pass the horse stables. Continue up the hill for another 0.8 miles and park on the right at the trailhead.

Looking Glass Falls

No hike necessary

Is there such a thing as "the classic waterfall"? Most people agree that Looking Glass Falls is the epitome of "a picture postcard" waterfall. Because of its easy access, Looking Glass Falls is a major tourist attraction, one of the most well-known falls in the eastern United States.

This waterfall is a symbol for the Pisgah National Forest. The cover of the Pisgah Area Trail Map sports a photo of Looking Glass Falls. The image shows up on many things you buy. You can even get a postcard of this "picture postcard" waterfall.

Holding rainwater like a sponge, the forest cover atop Looking Glass Rock gives rise to the creeks that feed the falls. The high volume from Looking Glass Creek creates an undivided rush of water, thirty-feet wide, that surges over a sixty-five-foot sheer drop. As the waters dive into the pool at the base, a misty spray drifts upward to coat the sides of the towering granite shelf.

Looking Glass Creek eventually flows into the Davidson River. The Davidson River south of Avery Creek is stocked from the nearby fish hatchery. In the early spring, you will find the streams busy with fisherman trying their luck for brook, brown, and rainbow trout. The hatchery raises and stocks sixty thousand trout in the streams of the Pisgah National Forest each year.

Many present-day highways in the Pisgah National Forest follow the old railroad beds of the by-gone era. US 276, the road past the falls, follows almost the exact location of an old railroad bed that transported timber out of the forest to the mills. In the early 1920's, the Carr Lumber Company built and maintained seventy-five miles of railroad in what is now the Pisgah National Forest.

For thirty years, lumber was one of the most thriving industries in Transylvania County. It was not uncommon to see three to four million board feet of lumber stacked around the Pisgah Forest Mill. The double-band mill was capable of sawing eighty to one hundred thousand board feet a day.

Directions: From the Pisgah Ranger Station in Pisgah Forest, travel 4 miles north on US 276. The parking area is on the right. You can observe the falls from your car or walk the steps to the base of the falls.

Moore Cove Falls

1.3 miles roundtrip, Easy

Moore Cove Falls could be an "all day-er"...not because it's a long hike...but because it's such a serene and restful spot, you could easily lose track of time. The gentle waters of Moore Creek dribble over a small series of stair-step ledges and then rain fifty-feet over a sheer drop to the creek below. The trail goes behind the docile curtain into a large granite cove. You can sit and look through the falling water without getting wet. It's like watching a summer rain through a window. The cool nook provides plenty of seating and could easily accommodate a group of friends.

The trail to the falls is a natural obstacle course—lots of diversity and lots of fun. The beginning of the trail meanders between house-sized granite boulders that are laced with veins of quartz. The boulders are covered with rhododendron and other assorted vegetation. Further along the trail there is a wooden slat bridge, soggy ground, and creek crossings, which require you to rock-hop and negotiate log bridges. Near the falls, you have to duck under a strange-looking tree, growing horizontally for twenty feet out of the side a hill before turning upward for another fifty feet.

The falls were named for Adam Q. Moore, a one-time U.S. Commissioner and justice of the peace. Moore owned fifty acres along Looking Glass Creek. Although he only owned the land for three years, his name was commonly used and became permanently attached to the creek and the falls. He sold his entire parcel in 1880 to the King family, who conveyed ownership to the Vanderbilt estate in 1901 for the modest sum of $155.

The trail follows Moore Creek to the falls. There is a small, primitive camping site just downstream within view of the falls. For those who like to fall asleep to the "pitter-patter" of rain, Moore Cove Falls could be your ticket to dreamland.

Directions: From the Pisgah Ranger Station in Pisgah Forest, go 5 miles north on US 276. Moore Cove Falls is 1 mile up the road from Looking Glass Falls. Park in the area beside the concrete bridge on the right of the road. Walk over the bridge to find the trailhead between the two wooden posts.

High Falls

4 miles roundtrip, Strenuous

High Falls is not....high! It is also not particularly wide, or powerful, or distinctive, or easy to access. But of all the things High Falls is "not," the most important virtue is that it's "not" frequently visited.

The trail can be confusing and you have to wade across South Mills River. Many people simply can't find the falls. This tranquil seclusion makes High Falls the ideal oasis for the urban hermit wishing to get away from it all.

One mile from the trailhead, go left on the small side trail just before the old concrete bridge. Continue 0.6 miles until you get to South Mills River. Ford the twenty-foot-wide river, which can be between one to three feet deep. Continuing 0.4 miles on the trail, you will pass a high waterfall dropping into the creek from the left, but this is not High Falls. Keep walking down the soggy trail a short distance to the actual High Falls.

You'll soon see the river gushing over a large jumble of rocks creating thirty feet of churning chaos. In sharp contrast to the agitated white water, there is a calm pool at the base—as big as a swimming pool.

Many grist mills and saw mills once graced the streams and rivers of these mountains, so it would be easy to conclude this was the derivation for the name South Mills River. Actually, the Revolutionary War veteran, Major William Mills, named the river after himself. In 1787, he was awarded 640 acres in return for his military service.

The headwaters of South Mills River meanders through the famous Pink Beds in the Pisgah National Forest. At an altitude of over thirty-two hundred feet, the Pink Beds are an unusual highland bog. The thirty-six square mile tract of land could have gotten it's name from the startling array of rosebay rhododendrons, mountain laurel, wild azaleas, and great masses of wild pink phlox—a botanist's paradise. Or, another source of the name could have been the pink rock that was once mined in the area.

Directions: From the Pisgah Ranger Station in Pisgah Forest, travel 10 miles north on US 276. Go right on FS 1206 (Yellow Gap Road) and follow the gravel road for 3.3 miles. Go right again on FS 476 (South

Mills River Road) and travel 1.3 miles to the end of the road. The trailhead leaves from the lower end of the parking area.

Waterfalls in Graveyard Fields

Upper Yellowstone Falls: 3.2 miles roundtrip, Easy
Second Falls: 0.8 miles roundtrip, Moderate

"Get Along Little Doggie," "Happy Trails to You," "The Wayward Wind".....it's easy to find yourself humming western songs on your way through Graveyard Fields. With a little imagination, you're convinced that you are in the West rather than a national forest in North Carolina. In contrast to the surrounding abundant timberland, the barren, rock-strewn landscape is only sparsely dotted with scraggly trees.

At an elevation of 5,120 feet, Graveyard Fields was named for its unique terrain. Fallen trees and stumps, which once blanketed the area, were covered with moss and spruce needles, resembled gravestones. A fire in 1925 destroyed twenty-five thousand acres, leaving a desolate open pocket of land, which has recovered slowly.

Follow the paved trail for 0.2 miles through a dense rhododendron thicket to the wooden bridge spaning the Yellowstone Prong of the Pigeon River's East Fork. The trail left leads to Upper Yellowstone Falls. The trail right leads to Second Falls.

The trail to Upper Yellowstone Falls follows Yellowstone Prong. While mostly flat, the path occasionally joins washed-out storm beds and is rocky in places. At trail's end, when you see a small current of rushing water, you may think "Is that it?" Cross over the channel and walk around the bend to view Upper Yellowstone Falls.

Yellowstone Prong emerges between two rock masses and pours fifty feet down a narrow stone channel. The towering rock wall, which directs the current, is not typical gray granite, but pale pink in color. The surrounding walls create a small canyon, adding to the western-type landscape.

Second Falls, also called Little Yellowstone Falls, is only 0.2 miles from the bridge over the Yellowstone Prong. The trail makes a sharp right

Second Falls on the Yellowstone Prong is as wide as 25 feet across and 60 feet tall. Photo by Nicole Blouin.

and descends steeply through an area washed out by drainage to the base of the falls. Second Falls is also visible from the Parkway before you reach Graveyard Fields Overlook.

The current is wider than Upper Yellowstone Falls and it drops over a series of three ledges for a total of sixty feet. As the water proceeds off the last ledge, it fans to a width of twenty-five feet. Unlike Upper Yellowstone Falls, the waters combine at the bottom to form an inviting swimming hole.

There is a third waterfall on Yellowstone Prong called Yellowstone Falls. It appears on some maps and in some reference material, but there is no maintained trail and the access is dangerously steep. According to forest rangers, it is not recommended.

Directions: From the Pisgah Ranger Station in Pisgah Forest, travel 13.4 miles north on US 276 to the Blue Ridge Parkway. Go south on the Parkway for 7.1 miles to Graveyard Fields Overlook (milepost 419). The trail leaves from the parking area down a wooden stairway.

Jackson Falls

1 mile roundtrip, Easy

Jackson Falls does not appear on any of the official trail maps because it was only discovered some twenty years ago. No one knew the falls existed until the early 1970s when Ray Jackson cut the logging road to access the timber management area south of Laurel Ridge. His co-workers started calling this waterfall Jackson Falls, and the name stuck.

Often waterfalls bear the name of the individual who owns the land or happens to discover the falls. In the case of this waterfall, the honor goes to the timber management administrator.

Jackson Falls begins its near-vertical descent down the mountainside one hundred feet above the logging road. It cascades, slides, leaps, and free-falls over a series of large stone slabs. The moderate volume of water begins as an eight-foot-wide branch and reaches a width of forty feet by the time it drops to the base. The waters run under the road and continue down the mountain, running into one of the prongs of the Davidson River.

A gravel logging road ascends a hill and leads to the base of Jackson Falls. To the left of the falls, there is a trail marker for Daniels Ridge Trail, a new name for an old trail. Thinking we could get a different view of the falls, we hiked the moderate 0.4-mile slope.

From the top, there was no view of the falls due to dense foliage, but the sound effects were great and there was an excellent view of Looking Glass Rock. With water streaming down its sides and reflecting the sunlight, Looking Glass Falls stands like a lonely sentinel, rising seventeen hundred feet above the forest floor. The Daniel Ridge Trail continues past the top of the falls into the timber management area.

Directions: From the Pisgah Ranger Station in Pisgah Forest, travel 3.5 miles north on US 276 and turn left onto FS 475 (Fish Hatchery Road). After 1.4 miles, you will pass the fish hatchery, the paved road changes to gravel. Take FS 475A, the lower gravel road that follows the river, for 1.9 miles. Continue past Cove Creek Campground for 0.7 miles to the unmarked parking circle on the right. Walk up the road past the gate for 0.5 miles. The falls will be on the left. (This is an active logging area so be sure not to block the locked forest service gate.)

18

Lake Toxaway

In the western part of Transylvania County, US 64 passes Lake Toxaway. Toxaway, taken from the Cherokee Indian word "Toxawah," which means "red bird," lies within the valley of Mount Toxaway in the southern Blue Ridge. The original town of Toxaway was actually incorporated in 1901 at the site of present-day Rosman. However, when Lake Toxaway was built and the area around the lake began to be developed, people began to get the two places confused. To make things easier, Joseph Silversteen changed the name of Toxaway to Rosman, in honor of two of his business associates, Mr. Rosenthal and Mr. Omansky.

The modern-day Lake Toxaway is a picture of tranquility. The glimmering surface of the water reflects the lush green of the surrounding forests and mirrors the sapphire blue of the sky. Nestled serenely among the mountains, gracious homes dot the perimeter of the lake.

Imagine, ladies and gentlemen in elegant attire stroll the beautiful shores of Lake Toxaway, while children roll playfully across the manicured lawns of the opulent Toxaway Inn. Couples in canoes skim lazily across the calm lake. Listen, and you can almost hear their refined voices carrying across the crisp mountain air, or the tinkle of crystal drifting through the open doors of the inn's tasteful dining room like musical notes.

Once, in this remote mountain valley was the "Switzerland of

America." The rich and famous came in droves, the guest list including such names as Edison, Ford, Vanderbilt, Firestone, Reynolds, and Rockefeller. This genteel civilization rode in on the rail, was swept away with a mighty roar, and was reborn on the shimmering waters of present-day Lake Toxaway. The story of how it happened is fascinating.

George Vanderbilt began it all when he built his Biltmore Estate near Asheville in the late 1800s. Suddenly, the remote mountain wilderness of western North Carolina was prime property. Soon, other northern entrepreneurs began to recognize the potential of the area and came to be part of the "boom." Among them were J. Frances Hayes and Joseph Silversteen.

Hayes conceived the idea of a resort for millionaires and set about building Lake Toxaway and the Toxaway Inn. He had the genius of foresight to purchase the Transylvania Railroad Company (formerly the Hendersonville & Brevard), for no resort could succeed without a comfortable means of transporting its guests. Transportation in those early days consisted of horse and ox-drawn wagons along a few questionable roads. Needless to say, the railroad was crucial to the success of Mr. Hayes's venture. In order to insure the passage of a bond issue to extend the railroad from Brevard to Lake Toxaway, Hayes agreed to build the Franklin Hotel in Brevard.

The rail line that began at Asheville and extended to Toxaway was not an easy feat. It was the steepest railroad system in the United States, but it was essential in transporting affluent tourists to the Toxaway Inn and other area resorts such as the Fairfield Inn, the Sapphire Inn, the Lodge, and the Franklin Hotel. Like the railroad, these magnificent resorts were outstanding accomplishments for their time.

Lake Toxaway was the first artificial lake ever built in the Appalachian Mountains; there was no other lake like it in the eastern United States. Its waters flowed from pure mountain springs and waterfalls of the surrounding unspoiled wilderness. Perched at 3,012 feet, this 640-acre lake, with fourteen miles of shoreline, was the largest man-made lake in the world at that time. The earthen dam that held the lake was five hundred feet long, sixty feet high, twenty feet wide at the top, and fifty feet thick at the base.

Toxaway Inn, opening in 1903, was an elegant resort, one of the finest of its era. It was built using more than forty species of wood, all cut from the property. It offered the rare modern conveniences of central heat, indoor plumbing, and elevators. French chefs prepared exquisite cuisine, served on imported china and crystal. Only the finest linens and silver were used. Guests danced the night away in the ballroom and found recreation in the billiard parlor and bowling alley. Those wishing sport could swim, boat, fish, hike, play tennis, or ride horseback.

A Southern Railroad brochure promoted Lake Toxaway as "...a lovely spot, high up in the glorious mountains of western North Carolina, and it will do you good to go there." Many wealthy people agreed. But when the Toxaway Inn was at the height of its splendor, the unpredictable hand of nature swept it all away with the flick of a wrist.

The rains came in the summer of 1916. Western North Carolina was severely flooded and the dam, having no low drainage pipe, was filled to capacity. In early August, a hurricane came ashore from the Gulf of Mexico and moved inland up the Mississippi Valley. The combination of rains from the hurricane and a smaller storm produced another deluge of unprecedented proportions.

The *Greenville News* of August 14, 1916, reported that, at 7:10 on the evening of August 13, the dam caved and sent a "solid wall of water thirty feet high" down the sixteen-mile gorge into South Carolina. It was said that the thunderous roar could be heard for miles.

Miraculously, accounts say the only loss of life was a blind mule. The destruction of property, however, was astronomical. Many of the area mills were obliterated as well. The damage suits and litigation lasted for years, mainly because there were those who indicated that the dam had been leaking prior to August 13th. It was also shown that the dam was built on top of a spring that had weakened the earthen structure.

Photographs taken around Toxaway Falls prior to the dam break show lush foliage and vegetation across the entire area. The force of an estimated five billion gallons of rushing water uprooted everything growing in its path, including trees four feet in diameter. Boulders the size of trucks were pitched down the gorge like marbles. The present-day site of Toxaway Falls is a three-hundred-foot-wide bare expanse of rock that drops 350 feet to the river below.

Although the Toxaway Inn was not destroyed, the disastrous loss of the lake spelled its demise. Added to the catastrophe of the dam break, World War I and the Great Depression contributed to the end of the tourist trade. Lake Toxaway was once again a quiet, secluded spot, hidden among the mountains. It would remain so for almost half a century.

The area was revived with the rebuilding of the dam and the lake in 1961. A group of investors, headed by R.D. Heinitsh, Sr., bought the nine thousand acre tract that had surrounded the original resort of Toxaway. The new dam, completed in March of 1961, was sixty feet deep and three hundred feet wide at the base with a solid granite spillway sixty feet wide. The Lake Toxaway Company also began the construction of roads around the lake.

While the Toxaway Inn no longer stands, the Greystone Inn graces the shores of Lake Toxaway as a reminder of the grandeur of that bygone era. Savannah native Lucy Armstrong Moltz spent a summer camping near Lake Toxaway before building this mansion—her second home—in 1915. "I've been around the world twice and I've found no place more beautiful or special," she wrote. In 1985, the home was opened as an inn—a six-level Swiss mansion offering award-winning accommodations.

In the interim between the flood and the rebuilding of Lake Toxaway, the area did not go completely unnoticed. The beauty of the scenery here inspired Hollywood to use the site as a film location. The movie *Tap Roots* with Susan Haywood and Van Heflin was filmed on location here in the 1948. The famous Robert Mitchum film *Thunder Road* was made here in 1957.

Lake Toxaway resident Jack Hall was seventeen years old at the time *Thunder Road* was filmed. He remembers playing hookey from school for two weeks in order to assist with the production. Jack vividly recalls the day they filmed the famous scene in which the '57 Ford crashed over the falls to the river below.

Only, according to Jack, the car didn't exactly fall where it was supposed to. Instead, the plunging vehicle landed to the right of the falls, setting the woods on fire. The wreckage lay there for months, giving souvenir seekers a chance to grab a piece of *Thunder Road*. Jack got the hood ornament and a door handle.

Today, Lake Toxaway is the largest private lake in North Carolina. The Lake Toxaway Company and Country Club are carrying on in the exclusive tradition of the Toxaway Inn, offering a luxurious standard of living in a secluded mountain setting. Once again, people come from all around to enjoy the splendor of the lake, the mountains, and the forests.

Fortunately, the majestic mountains and lush forest belong to all of us. They are ours to cherish, along with the region's coursing rivers and streams—the patrons of the waterfalls. Within a radius of a few miles of Lake Toxaway, there are dozens of waterfalls (three that can be visited at Lake Toxaway Country Estates).

Toxaway Falls

No hike necessary

"Wow, look at that!" is a common reaction from unsuspecting motorists, driving along US 64 between Sapphire and Brevard, who round the corner and see Toxaway Falls. Though the volume of water is low compared to some of the other falls in Transylvania County, the view of the falls and the river gorge below is spectacular. After a full day of waterfall trekking, the tired hiker may also appreciate that Toxaway Falls is visible from the car.

From the dam which impounds Lake Toxaway, the Toxaway River runs under the concrete bridge and the falls begin their near-vertical plunge at three thousand feet above sea level. Water slides 125 feet over a massive dome-shaped granite shelf, and halfway down, a curved rock causes the current to spout upward and form a huge rooster tail. The Toxaway River continues its turbulent path over numerous cascades and cataracts on its fifteen-hundred-foot descent through the picturesque Toxaway River Gorge, finally relaxing upon reaching the backwaters of Lake Jocassee.

Many people believe that the falls, river, mountain, and lake were named after the famous Cherokee Indian leader, Toxawah. The name

Toxaway Falls was once surrounded by lush vegetation. A dam break on Toxaway Lake above caused by a flood in 1916 cleared a 300-foot-wide path and exposed the massive granite dome below the soil. Photo by Ben Keys.

Toxaway was also linked to an Indian settlement in the area; however, the spelling on the old maps and deeds was "Toxawah." Prevailing legend puts the grave of Toxaway at the top of Indian Grave Ridge, which is approximately one quarter of a mile from the top of Toxaway Falls.

The rein of destruction from the fateful day of the flood of 1916 is still visible. The sweeping torrent cleared the heavy riverside vegetation and exposed the massive granite domes. The landscape may be altered, but the view from the top of the falls is still breathtaking.

Directions: Toxaway Falls is just downstream from Lake Toxaway Dam. US 64 goes over the top of the falls. Use the restaurant parking lot just west of the falls for a good view, or use an access point just east of the falls and walk out on the boulders for a closer view—extreme caution is advised.

Frozen Creek Shoals

0.4 miles roundtrip, Moderate

For the contemporary adventure seeker, Frozen Creek Shoals is an interesting waterfall with an interesting history. For yesterday's residents of the Ridge Haven Area, the Shoals was more—the power for a tub mill that was a means of making a living and providing for the family. For others, the Shoals provided "many a gallon for some of the finest bootleg whiskey known in these here parts."

After purchasing fifty acres on Frozen Creek in 1876, Jim Earl Galloway built a tub mill at the foot of the large shoal to grind corn. A wooden flume was constructed to carry water from the top of the falls to the awaiting turbines below. A tub mill, as opposed to a water wheel mill, accumulates the flow in a large tub, and then drains the water out the bottom through the turbines. As the water turns the turbines, a system of gears and rods turn the grinding stones which mill the corn into meal for farmers or mash for moonshiners.

In addition to serving as the major ingredient of the proud and potent product, the crystal-clear water was funneled through the still to aid in the fermentation process. The area became famous for the quality of its moonshine and was a major destination for those who preferred to "get their corn from a jar."

In 1924, a Rosman businessman named Dewey Winchester bought the fifty-five acre tract on Frozen Creek, including the old Galloway Mill. A short distance downstream from the mill, he dammed Frozen Creek to form Frozen Lake and constructed Frozen Lake Lodge.

Frozen Creek got its name because it runs along the west side of a mountain called Frozen Knob, which during winter is often glazed with ice. The site was once known as Mill Shoals, but because this name was so common throughout the county, the name was changed to Frozen Creek Shoals.

A short trail, which winds behind a private home, leads to Frozen Creek Shoals. Frozen Creek drains over a thirty-five foot high slanting granite shelf, forming the falls. Half-way down the ledge, the flow is partially obstructed by a rock ledge, creating a small rooster tail of water which protrudes off the rock face. The spirited waters quickly settle into a pool at the base where you can see the remnants of the gristmill and its stone foundation. From the lake, Frozen Creek flows into Toxaway Creek on its way to the Toxaway River and Lake Jocassee.

Directions: From Lake Toxaway Dam on US 64 (the location of Toxaway Falls), drive east 6.1 miles and go right onto Frozen Creek Road. After 0.7 miles, bear left and continue for another 3.3 miles. When you see a large wooden-framed home on the right, park on the road's shoulder. You'll hear the waters roar from the roadway, and the ill-defined trailhead is midway between the two telephone poles. (This is private property so permission should be sought if possible.)

Deep Ford Falls

1.2 miles roundtrip, Easy

Deep Ford Creek spills seventy-five feet over an unusual granite formation along the southeast side of Mount Toxaway. Deep Ford Falls is also called Crevice Cliff Falls because there is a huge cleft in the immense granite ledge that was formed by the convergence of molten masses millions of years ago. The sparse waters pour over a vertical, lichen-covered ledge to the left of the crevice and form a small pool at the bottom.

Before the area was developed, Deep Ford Falls was just one of the many waterfalls running off Mount Toxaway—known only to the locals. Today it is part of the Lake Toxaway Country Club. The country club sports a golf course, a 640-acre lake, the Greystone Inn, and numerous homes. While the grounds of the country club are finely manicured, a few dozen steps into this "country-club trail" reveals modern development stops at the road.

On the trail, nature remains untouched by the hand of "progress." Meandering through the woods, the trail follows—and then becomes part of—a rocky streambed. When you get to the falls, there is one obvious indication that this is an oft-visited spot. An appropriately placed picnic table rewards hikers with a perfect setting for an outdoor meal. So bring a picnic to feed your body while the surrounding beauty feeds your senses.

While the development of Lake Toxaway Country Club is quite appealing, there have been many changes over the years. During the 1930s and 1940s, Mount Toxaway was heavily logged and the road to Deep Ford Falls went through the middle of the current-day Lake Toxaway. The roads were so steep that the logging trucks had to be pulled up and let down by bulldozers and cables. Winding Stairs Road was infamous with its grade of fifty to fifty-five degrees—a real test of endurance for the loggers. Remnants of the road are still visible.

During the 1960s, tens of thousands of board-feet of the extremely rare wormy chestnut logs were harvested along the side of Mount Toxaway. Killed by the blight in the 1930s, the chestnut trees fell and settled into low-lying wet areas. After becoming saturated they were called "sog logs" and invading worms would eat their way through the entire log. This worm-eaten, naturally distressed chestnut wood, used for furniture and paneling, is one of the rarest and most valuable of woods.

The name Mount Toxaway was given to the mountain that the locals called Hogback Mountain. While the mountain was supposedly named because it resembled the sloping back of a hog, we prefer the version suggested by local realtor Jack Hall.

"I can remember riding with Granddaddy Fisher along old roads in his horse-drawn wagon searching for his hogs. This was before the stock-up laws of the 1950s, when everyone let their domestic animals roam free. The hogs would always wind up at the foot of Deep Ford Falls. Granddaddy would throw out some corn and start calling the hogs. They'd come running to us when called just like a dog would. We had a pit bull named Old Jerry and after we picked out which hogs we wanted, Old Jerry would wrestle the hog to the ground and hold it until Granddaddy Fisher could tie it. We would then put the hogs in the wagon and go home. Deep Ford Falls and Hogback Mountain was where we went to get our "hogs back.'"

Directions: From Lake Toxaway Dam on US 64 (the location of Toxaway Falls), drive west for 0.9 miles to Lake Toxaway Country Club. Turn right into the main entrance; there is a guard here during the summer months. State that you are going to the falls, they are open to the public. Go 1.8 miles along this residential road (West Club Boulevard) to the trailhead on the left side of the road.

Little Deep Ford Falls

No hike necessary

Dropping to the road from one hundred feet, Little Deep Ford Falls is anything but "little." The name might suggest that the falls are a miniature version of Deep Ford Falls (see previous waterfall entry) but this is not the case. The falls are named for the feeder creek—Little Deep Ford Creek.

This stream, along with Mill Creek and Big Deep Ford Creek, make up the watershed running off Mount Toxaway. All three creeks, plus the Toxaway River, flow into Lake Toxaway.

High on a mountainside, a private home sits nestled into the dense foliage adjacent to the top of Little Deep Ford Falls. A few yards from the overlooking deck, Little Deep Ford Creek emerges, dropping into a small pool. The waters gather and form a larger overflow which free-falls before disappearing from view. Thirty-feet to the right, the waters reappear and pour over a large granite wall, forming two long cascades that descend to the road.

The Lake Toxaway Company, an environmentally conscious developer, built a mountain oasis for the city-weary, while preserving the natural beauty of the surrounding area. The road running along the base of the cascade was carefully cut by the developers to showcase the beauty of Little Deep Ford Falls, which overlooks the second fairway of the golf course.

Directions: From Lake Toxaway Dam on US 64 (the location of Toxaway Falls), travel to Lake Toxaway Country Club (see directions under Deep Ford Falls). Continue 0.3 miles past the trailhead for Deep Ford Falls and go left on Chestnut Trace. Follow Chestnut Trace for 0.5 miles. Little Deep Ford Falls is on the left side of the road. There is a parking shoulder on the right opposite the falls.

Mill Creek Falls

0.4 miles roundtrip, Easy

Before the formation of Lake Toxaway, Mill Creek plummeted a total of 730 feet in a half mile as it raced between Raven Rock Mountain and Mount Toxaway (also known as Hogback Mountain). Today, a humble reminder of its former fury can be observed in Mill Creek Falls, which tumbles eighty-five feet over a series of bold granite ledges. The gushing water drops freely, slides over a huge rock ledge, free-falls again, then cascades over another granite outcropping before forming a calm pool at the base.

The falls and the creek were formally known as McKinney Creek and McKinney Falls, named after landowner James McKinney. A gristmill was built at the base of the falls and "Slick" Fisher was the last mill operator. Over time the name evolved into Mill Creek to identify with the mill.

Mill Creek Falls served as a weather barometer for the hardy pioneers that inhabited the area in the early days. Families living within earshot of the falls knew "bad weather was a-comin'" when the roar from the falls increased. Jack Hall, a local resident and realtor, remembers in the early eighties when the entire creekbed froze over and ice that formed at the base of the falls was twenty to thirty feet thick.

The short trail to the falls is along a narrow wooded path. The falls can be heard long before they come into view.

Directions: From the Lake Toxaway Dam on US 64 (the location of Toxaway Falls), see the directions under Little Deep Ford Falls. Continue on Chestnut Trace another 0.3 miles and go left on Fairway Drive. Go 0.8 miles to the trailhead on the left side of the road. Park on the shoulder of the road.

19

Cashiers

Cashiers appears to be just a crossroads, the junction of US 64 and NC 107. Here, you'll find the only traffic light in town. But there is much more to this quiet resort town than the intersection of these two highways.

Located on the eastern Continental Divide at 3,486 feet, Cashiers is surrounded by twenty thousand acres of national forest—the Nantahala National Forest and the Pisgah National Forest. For every ten acres of forest, there is one acre of lake, including Lake Glenville, which is considered to be the highest major lake in the East.

There are several peaks that rise fifteen hundred feet above the town. The highest, Yellow Mountain, stands at 5,127 feet above sea level. Cashiers also claims the famous Whiteside Mountain, sharing it with Highlands even though the mountain is a couple of miles closer to Cashiers. For a great photograph, take US 64 west out of town for four miles (before the Jackson County line) and pull over on the right. This area, known as Big View, offers an astounding picture-postcard view of Whiteside Mountain.

If you're interested in history, there are two rocks that are worth a visit—Judaculla Rock and Ellicott's Rock. Judaculla Rock, located on Caney Fork Road, is a forty-foot boulder with pictographs. These symbols may have been carved by Indians, but they have yet to be deciphered. Ellicott's Rock, named for Andrew Ellicott who surveyed the

Whitewater Falls, at 411 feet, is the highest cascade east of the Rockies. Photo by Nicole Blouin.

line between North Carolina and South Carolina around 1812, marks the junction of Georgia, South Carolina, and North Carolina. This rock can be reached via the Ellicott Rock Trail (seven miles roundtrip) at Ammons Branch Campground.

The attractive shops and fine restaurants of Cashiers are similar to Highlands—antiques and made-in-Carolina crafts, country food and gourmet cuisine—except there are not as many and they are not as crowded. If you only have a little time to shop, go to the Cashiers Country Store, located on NC 107 just south of the town's main intersection. One stop provides all the mountain treasures you can imagine—homemade goodies, custom-made quilts, and North Carolina pottery. There is even a Christmas room open year-round.

Usually, you find crowds in Cashiers only during one of the festivals. At the "Celebration of Mountain Spring" in May, you can tour historic inns and enjoy local music and art. In the summer, there's "Pioneer Day," a historic celebration of the founding of the town. You can dance in the street, participate in field events, and eat barbecue.

Cashiers has an unusual name, and there are an unusually large number of theories about the origin. There is also a long-standing controversy about which theory is right. The valley could have been named after a lumber company cashier's office or after an original settler who lived in the area, but the stories that involve animals seem to be more popular.

Some people think there was a horse named "Cash" who wandered off and a search party yelled "Cash's here" when they found him. Others believe it was a race horse whose prize money earned him the right to spend winters in the valley instead of heading south with the rest of the stock. Change horse to bull, and "Cash" to "Cassius," and you have yet another story about how Cashiers got its name.

The list of theories is long and there doesn't seem to be a consensus. So, here are the facts. Cashiers was settled around 1830 by Colonel John Zachary and James McKinney; but records mention the area as early as 1540 when Hernando de Soto, the Spanish explorer, came through on his way to the Mississippi River.

The Cherokee Indians were here for several generations before the first settlers (Scots and Irish) put up their log cabins in the early 1800s. At the turn of this century, many of the South's elite came to Cashiers to escape the heat, and the town's been slowly growing as a resort area ever since. One such summer resident, General Wade Hampton from South Carolina, had a home on Chimney Mountain, which is now the High Hampton Inn and Country Club, one of North Carolina's most exclusive resorts.

Every town has its claim to fame, some have several. My favorite piece of Cashiers trivia involves the Grimshawes post office, which is the smallest (six by eight) post office in the United States. You can visit the restored building on Whiteside Cove Road.

Cashiers has another claim to fame; it is home to one of the highest waterfalls in the East. It is spectacular, but as you'll discover, the other waterfalls around Cashiers won't be upstaged. Don't miss the hike along the Wild and Scenic Horsepasture River or the boat trip to the waterfalls on Lake Glenville.

Whitewater Falls

0.4 miles roundtrip, Easy

This is the king of waterfalls; it is considered to be the highest cascade east of the Rockies. Whitewater Falls lives up to its title. It is immense, it is spectacular. The river plunges 411 feet over the sheer granite cliffs of the gorge; it falls, tumbles, and slides. The ground seems to shake as the sound of crashing water echoes in the valley.

Silver Run Creek (where you will find Silver Run Falls) and Little Whitewater Creek join above Whitewater Falls to form the Whitewater River. After the river crosses the border of North Carolina and South Carolina, it drops another four hundred feet, creating Lower Whitewater Falls, and then flows into Lake Jocassee.

Whitewater Falls is surrounded by a mix of oak, poplar, maple, and hickory. The highlights of the understory are thimbleberry and woodland sunflower. The constant spray from the falls creates a home for several tropical ferns and mosses.

You can enjoy the falls from an observation point at the end of the paved walkway and then head back to the picnic tables for lunch and a great view of Lake Jocassee. Or, if you have more time, you can reach the base of the falls by exploring a portion of the Foothills Trail that intersects Whitewater Falls Scenic Area at the observation point. The Foothills Trail is an eighty-mile path stretching from Table Rock State Park to Oconee State Park. Simply descend the four hundred steps to the Whitewater River and head upstream.

Directions: Take NC 107 south for 7.2 miles to South Carolina; go another 1 mile and turn left onto 37-413 at the sign for Whitewater Falls. Follow it 2.2 miles to the stop sign and turn left again. After you cross into North Carolina, drive 0.2 miles and turn left at the sign for Whitewater Falls Scenic Area. Follow this 0.3-mile access road to the parking area. The paved trail begins just beyond the information board and chemical toilets.

Falls on the Horsepasture River

Drift Falls: 0.2 miles roundtrip, Moderate
Turtleback Falls: 0.8 miles roundtrip, Moderate
Rainbow Falls: 1.2 miles roundtrip, Moderate
Stairway Falls: 2.8 miles roundtrip, Strenuous

Prior to October 27th, 1986, the Horsepasture River was in danger because a power company was planning to build a hydroelectric dam that would terminate the water flow to the falls. But FROTH (Friends of the Horsepasture River), with the help of legislators and state organizations, won their fight to block the project. Four and one-half miles of the river was designated Wild and Scenic to be protected by the federal government.

The river is wild; it plunges almost two thousand feet over six miles in a dramatic series of wide drops and boulder-filled rapids. The river is scenic; the banks are covered with rhododendrons and hemlocks, and the rare shortia plant can be found here on occasion.

The river is a waterfall collector's heaven; four outstanding cascades can be seen along this trail. During the first hundred yards or so, you must climb over small boulders and struggle with tree roots and branches; but the main portion of trail is well-maintained and relatively flat.

It is common to see swimmers enjoying Drift Falls in the summer. The locals call it Bohaynee Beach named after the nearby community. There are some adventuresome characters that ride the falls like a commercial super-slide, sailing over rocks on inner-tubes. The river glides over an enormous dome into a calm swimming hole; the total drop is thirty feet. I wouldn't recommend the ride, but you can sure stop and enjoy the show.

Turtleback Falls only drops twenty feet, but the surrounding area is beautiful. The river takes a ninety-degree right turn. Upstream of the curve, you'll find the falls, a river-wide, uniform drop over a smooth shelf. Downstream of the curve, just beyond some big boulders, the river disappears.

In actuality, the Horsepasture's vanishing act is Rainbow Falls, a near-vertical drop of two hundred feet. The entire river crashes onto the boulders below, producing a deafening roar. If the sun is just right, you may see colorful arches created in the spray; hence the name, Rainbow Falls.

Few people venture as far as Stairway Falls because the trail becomes more difficult and overgrown in places. After you cross a ten-foot wide creek, hike several hundred yards uphill and locate the side trail (sharp right) that leads down to the river.

The peaceful nature of the falls is captivating, quite a change from the powerful Rainbow Falls. Several stair-steps, averaging ten feet each, add up to a total drop of just over fifty feet. At one time, it was called Adam Shoals, after a previous owner. His wife is buried to the east of the falls. Her death (in 1879) is puzzling. The coroner stated that she fell into the fireplace of their home, but how she fell is unknown.

Directions: Travel east from Cashiers on US 64 for about 9 miles to NC 281 and turn right. After 1.8 miles, pull off alongside the guardrail on the extended shoulder on the left. If you cross the bridge over the

Horsepasture River, you have gone too far. There are several places to scramble down and intersect the ungraded trail that parallels the river.

Waterfalls of Lake Glenville

No hike necessary

Tired of hiking? Here are three waterfalls—Hurricane Falls, Norton Falls, and Mill Creek Falls—that you can visit by boat. What kind of boat? You name it! Take a canoe or a sailboat, a wave runner or a ski boat. David Johnston and Jim Roberts have a marina on Lake Glenville and will be glad to give you a map, rent you a boat, and help you plan a day of sightseeing.

Each waterfall is located on a different finger of the lake and cascades about thirty or forty feet, depending on the lake's level. Hurricane Falls is two miles south of the marina, and Norton Falls and Mill Creek Falls are two and four miles north, respectively. With a pontoon boat, you can see all three in a couple of hours. With a canoe, it's feasible to paddle to either Norton Falls or Hurricane Falls.

While you're out, explore one of the islands or sunbathe on one of the natural sand beaches. Fishing is also popular. The lake is exceptionally clean because it is at the top of the watershed and fed by springs. At an elevation of thirty-five hundred feet, this 1,462-acre lake creates twenty-six miles of shoreline.

Lake Glenville Thorpe Reservoir was formed when a dam was built on the West Fork of the Tuckasegee River. The project was in response to the power requirements of World War II. Each day, the plant generated enough electricity to produce aluminum for two B-17 Flying Fortress bombers. The lake recently turned fifty years old; power went on-line in October of 1941.

Directions: Leave Cashiers heading north towards Glenville on NC 107. Travel 5 miles to Jim's Landing on the left. David and Jim practically live at the marina between Memorial Day and Labor Day. If you visit the area during the off-season, be sure to call ahead for a reservation. The phone number is 704-743-2095.

The twenty five foot tall Silver Run Falls drops into an inviting swimming hole. Photo by John Newman.

Silver Run Falls

0.4 miles roundtrip, Easy

On my first visit to Silver Run Falls, my step-daughter Alison Jones accompanied me. Writing has always been one of her favorite hobbies and she wants to major in English Education when she goes off to college this fall. I offered her this section and without hesitation she said, "Yes." Here's what she came up with for this waterfall.

The trail to Silver Run Falls is almost completely level. Half-way to the falls, you must cross a small creek on a natural foot bridge, which is formed by a fallen hemlock tree. Just downstream, the small creek joins Silver Run Creek. These two creeks are part of the headwaters of the Whitewater River, where you'll find Whitewater Falls.

If you follow the sound of rushing water for several hundred yards, the trail will bring you out to a rock that is perfect for viewing this twenty-five foot falls. The blue-green water pours into a large, circular pool creating an inviting swimming hole. From the small sandy beach, two downed trees can be used to walk across the pool for a better photo angle. Silver Run Falls is surrounded by a damp forest of rhododendron, hemlock, and poplar.

Directions: Drive south from Cashiers on NC 107 for 3.5 miles where you will see trash dumpsters on the left. Travel another 0.5 miles to the second pull-off on the left after the dumpsters. The trailhead is at the utility pole.

20

Highlands

ighlands is an elegant mountain town. Main Street is lined with fashionable boutiques, fine restaurants, and exquisite specialty shops. Even the gas stations are attractive; it is difficult to find a chain store. A stroll around downtown Highlands is almost as much fun as a hike to one of the area's magnificent waterfalls.

Until 1981, when the community of Beech Mountain was incorporated, Highlands was considered the highest town east of the Mississippi. The average elevation is 4,118 feet. The Cherokee named this high land "Onteeoorah," which translates loosely to "hill of sky."

The surrounding peaks range from 4,200 to 5,000 feet. The most famous, Whiteside Mountain, boasts sheets of granite ranging in height from 400 to 750 feet. From the summit at five thousand feet, you can see for fifty miles in every direction.

Besides being one of the highest towns in the Blue Ridge, Highlands has almost as much rainfall as the western slopes of Oregon and Washington. The average annual rainfall is almost eighty inches. This abundant water feeds the headwaters of the Chattooga River and the Cullasaja River. There are also springs on almost every acre—nearly two hundred within the town boundaries.

Add the altitude and rainfall to Highland's lack of polluting industry or agriculture, and the result is a special place, unique and diverse in its flora and fauna. From Wilson Gap Road, you can visit the second largest poplar tree in the East. To find out more about the area's plants and animals, go to the Highland's Nature Center on Horse Cove Road.

The Nature Center is open from Memorial Day to Labor Day. You can walk through the botanical gardens, listen to films and archaeological lectures, and let the kids attend educational classes. A group of citizens founded the Nature Center in 1927 to create a place for a display of plants, animals, minerals, and Indian artifacts. Over the years, hundreds of papers have been published based on the research performed here.

If you're lucky enough to be in the area in December when there's snow on the ground, head for Scaly Mountain, located seven miles southwest of Highlands on NC 106. You can ski any of four runs, which are rated for beginner through advanced, and then enjoy the "little" Christmas parade put on by this small community of three hundred.

There is an interesting story behind the founding of Highlands. Legend tells of two land developers from Kansas, Samuel Truman Kelsey and Clinton Carter Hutchinson, who marked a spot on a map by drawing a line from Chicago to Savannah, and from New Orleans to Baltimore. They theorized that the intersection of these two lines would someday become a commercial mecca. The "X" marked the area of present-day Highlands.

Kelsey and Hutchinson purchased 839 acres from Captain J.W. Dobson of Horse Cove. The proposed settlement was established on March 30, 1875. But because the mountains were too steep for trains, and the mules were too slow, the initial dream of a great population center quickly faded. Yet the two men saw the magic in this place and set about promoting their new town.

As early as 1896, Kelsey and Hutchinson advertised Highlands as a health resort; the high altitude, a curative for many diseases like yellow fever, which plagued the low country of the Carolinas. Their brochures boasted unsurpassed beauty, along with few flies and no mosquitoes. The area's waterfalls were also used in promotion; publications told of the spectacular cascades of the Cullasaja River and other "falls too numerous to mention."

Kelsey and Hutchinson didn't exaggerate. The cascades of the Cullasaja River are spectacular, and the area's waterfalls are too numerous to mention. Here are a few to get you started. Stop in at the Forest Service Visitor Information Center on the west side of town (before the junction of US 64 and NC 106) and ask about Secret Falls, Flat Creek Falls, and others.

Glen Falls

2 miles roundtrip, Strenuous

This is a three-for-the-price-of-one waterfall. It has three tiers, each sixty feet high and viewed separately from different spur trails. However, the price is high because the trail is steep, descending almost seven hundred feet in a mile. The trip out is tough. The trail is a little rough in places, but at the time of this writing, it was being re-worked to include additional wooden steps and better markers for the spur trails.

The falls, collectively known as Glen Falls, are located on the East Fork of Overflow Creek. Several spurs off the main trail give you a close-up look at the individual cascades. The first observation point, at the top of the first tier, is only ten minutes into the hike. From here, it looks like the falls are one huge drop. There are two other platforms beyond this point.

If 180 feet of falling water isn't enough, the Glen Falls Trail provides other splendid features. The vistas of the Blue Valley are exceptional. There are mature stands of pitch and white pine along the ridge above the falls, and vertical hillsides are covered with hardwoods and conifers. You will also find choice picnic sites near the beginning of the trail.

Directions: From Highlands, head west on US 64 to the junction of US 64 and NC 106. Go south on NC 106 for 1.7 miles and turn left at the sign for Glen Falls Scenic Area. This road is gravel and ends at a parking area after 1 mile. The trailhead is just beyond the information board. Be sure to take the trail to the left. (Chinquapin Mountain Trail is to the right.)

Waterfalls of the Cullasaja Gorge

Kalakaleskies Falls: 0.1 miles roundtrip, Moderate
Bridal Veil Falls: No hike necessary
Dry Falls: 0.3 miles roundtrip, Easy
Lower Cullasaja Falls: No hike necessary

The Cullasaja Gorge is a masterpiece. It would be difficult to find a more rugged river gorge anywhere in the Blue Ridge. US 64 and the Cullasaja River run parallel between Highlands and Franklin.

The road—a tourist's delight or an engineer's nightmare? Considered one of the most scenic routes in western North Carolina, this highway was carved into the side of a cliff. It winds wildly and closely follows the course of the river.

In order to build the road, workers were repeatedly lowered from cliff tops in rope slings to drill holes and place dynamite. They blasted away solid granite. Construction began in 1928; and in 1929, an estimated two thousand people attended a ceremony to unveil a monument to the town's founder, Samuel Kelsey. The first gravel was unloaded in 1931 and the road was partially paved by 1932.

It's a wonder the work was ever completed. Funds were denied by the federal government because of the extreme expense, and delays came from the road department because they were not enthusiastic about starting the hardest project of their careers.

Fortunately, the road was constructed, or most of us would never get to witness the Cullasaja River's unspoiled beauty and tremendous power. Stating that the river descends two thousand feet in 7.5 miles should tell the story, but here's more. There are ripples and rapids, twist and turns, and...drops. These drops add up to several major falls and a dozen minor ones. They are sisters, but each one has a unique personality.

Just below the dam on Lake Sequoyah at the upper end of the Gorge, there is a series of small waterfalls called the Kalakaleskies. Scramble down the bank to the river's edge and explore. Within a quarter mile, there are eighteen small cascades. Some fall five feet, others forty. This is the beginning of the many waterfalls on the Cullasaja River.

The dam was built in 1927 and measures 28' X 175'. It creates the seventy-six-acre lake named after the famed Indian Chief, Sequoyah. This hunter and fur trader, who never attended school, developed a system of writing that enabled the Cherokees to read books and newspapers published in their own language. Sequoyah is the only Indian with a place in the Hall of Fame in Washington D.C.

The next waterfall comes with a legend. Indian maidens believed if they walked behind the falls in the spring, they would marry before the first snowfall. Thus, the name—Bridal Veil.

Bridal Veil is a delicate falls, the water volume is small. The upper section clings to an eighty-foot rock face and the lower section free-falls forty feet. Bridal Veil Falls blooms in the winter, when frozen spray adorns the plants, and icicles cling to the overhang.

Because this waterfall is just one hundred feet off the highway, it is the most well-known and photographed waterfall around Highlands. Traffic was routed along the paved semi-circle behind the falls before the construction of US 64.

Dry Falls boasts a very dry backside, which is where it gets its name, and its popularity. It is possible to walk under the falls without getting wet because a hollow area has been cut away by centuries of erosion. You can look out into the Blue Valley through the sheets of water.

A set of steps and a paved walkway will takes you to the viewing area. The river plunges seventy-five feet from a protruding rock shelf onto rocks just a few feet from the path. Rare plants, such as Rock Club Moss and Appalachian Filmy Fern, are watered by the constant spray. There is a sensational roar.

Don't turn back to Highlands until you've seen the last major waterfall in the Gorge. It is a blockbuster. Lower Cullasaja Falls is higher and more captivating than any of her sisters.

This waterfall crashes through the steep canyon over a series of wide ledges and then falls freely for 150 feet. The river splits into several dramatic cascades, each worthy of its own name. Dropping a total of 250 feet in one quarter mile, Lower Cullasaja Falls is considered one of the most picturesque falls in North Carolina.

The best vantage point is from a paved shoulder off US 64. A 0.5-

Lower Cullasaja Falls crashes through the canyon on a series of steep ledges and then falls freely for 150 feet. Photo by Nicole Blouin.

mile trail will get you closer; but it is difficult, and downed trees obscure the falls. Fortunately, the view from the shoulder is stunning. This may not be a perfect place for a picnic, but your photograph is sure to be striking.

Directions: From Highlands, head west on US 64 towards Franklin. Within 2 miles you will be driving alongside Sequoyah Lake and then the dam will be visible on the left. Kalakaleskies cover 0.25 miles below the dam and there are several places to stop. Bridal Veil Falls is next on your right. There is a paved circular pull-off. Travel another 0.9 miles to the parking area for Dry Falls on your left. And finally, pull off on the shoulder after 5.5 miles to view Lower Cullasaja Falls. There is not a sign to mark the area, but you can't miss the falls. You may have to turn around and come back to park.

Lower Satulah Falls

No hike necessary

If you are traveling to Highlands from Walhalla, South Carolina, or if you are just interested in a pleasant drive, don't miss Satulah Falls. Also called Clear Creek Falls, it can be seen from an overlook on NC 28.

Although the falls is about a quarter mile away, you can hear the sound of rushing water from the overlook. I'd advise a fairly long lens in order to capture this sixty-foot, sliding falls on film. But the photographic opportunities are not limited to the cascade; views of Rabun Bald and the Blue Valley are also possibilities.

After you leave the overlook and head into town, you will see the landmark cliffs on the south side of Satulah Mountain, a large rock outcropping with an elevation of 4,560 feet. In 1909, thirty-two acres of this mountain were purchased with monies raised by a few concerned citizens as an everlasting gift to the public.

Directions: From Highlands, head south on NC 28 towards Walhalla, and travel 3.6 miles to a large gravel pull-off on the right with wooden railings. The falls are straight ahead on the opposite slope.

21

Cherokee

Cherokee is more than a place, it is also a people. You can not understand the town of Cherokee without understanding the story of the Cherokee Indian. You may come to the town of Cherokee expecting to see tepees and painted warriors in feathered headdresses. And you will see those things—an illusion for the benefit of the tourist. But there is more to this place and these people.

The Cherokee were actually a sophisticated tribe who lived in structures made from wood, grass, and clay. They believed in a supreme being—the Great Spirit—and they believed in an afterlife.

The spirit, the very essence of the Cherokee Indian, is intrinsically tied to the Smoky Mountains of which he is a part. In fact, it is because of the mountains that the Cherokee Indian Reservation, known as the Qualla Boundary, exists today. The Cherokee, who refused to be forced from their homeland by the cruel Removal Act of 1830, took harbor in the heart of the Shaconage, "the place of blue smoke."

Long before white explorers came to the Blue Ridge, there were Indians here. Ethnologists generally believe that these natives began moving south nearly one thousand years ago, settling in the Appalachians between Ohio and South Carolina. The very birthplace of the Cherokee Indian was in the Smokies. Kituwha, the first Cherokee town, was located near Deep Creek Campground.

The Indians settled in the fertile valleys and beside the rivers at the foot of the mountains. They fished the streams and hunted the forests. They were mostly a peace-loving people, who lived in harmony with their surroundings. As an agricultural society, the Cherokee lived off the land.

The mountains provided their material resources, as well as their spiritual sustenance. The Cherokee believed that the "Little People" lived in the shadows of the mountains and kept the history of the tribe. Once a year, the tribe's wise men spent a week deep within the mountain forests to share legends with the "Little People," thereby preserving Cherokee heritage.

When the Spanish explorer Hernando de Soto encountered the Cherokee in 1540, he found a well-developed, unified, and gentle nation of approximately twenty-five thousand people. They had an organized form of government and were the first of all the Indian tribes in North America to have a written form of language, invented by Sequoyah in the 1820s.

Considered to be one of the most intelligent Indians in history, Sequoyah is the only person on record with the distinction of having designed an entire alphabet. It took him twelve years to create the system of symbols. Two years after he presented his alphabet to the Cherokee Council, *The Cherokee Phoenix* began circulation and nearly everyone who spoke Cherokee could read and write.

With exploration came the inevitable influx of settlers. Battles ensued over fur trade and land possession. During different periods of history, the Cherokee were both friend and foe to the white man. For example, they fought with the troops of General Andrew Jackson against the Creek Indians at the Battle of Horseshoe Bend in 1814. This loyalty was not rewarded, however, as it was President Jackson who signed the Act that forced the Indians westward.

The discovery of gold in the area sounded the death knell for the Cherokee. Greedy settlers, not content to share the land, continued to force the Indians out. Continuing the tragic undertaking that Jackson had begun, President Martin Van Buren, in 1838, ordered General Winfield Scott to enforce the removal of all the Cherokee to land west of the Mississippi (now Oklahoma). Between seventeen and twenty thousand Cherokee were rounded up and driven west over the "Trail of

Tears." An estimated one-fourth of the Indians died along the way from starvation, exposure, disease, and despair. One account from a government participant described it as "the cruelest work I ever knew."

About one thousand Cherokee fled to the isolation of the mountains, mostly to the areas of Swain, Jackson, and Haywood counties of North Carolina. Tsali was one of these Cherokee refugees who was hiding his family. He had killed a soldier who mistreated his wife during the disastrous march west. Tsali's hiding place is believed to have been somewhere along what is now the Thomas Divide Trail in the Great Smoky Mountains National Park.

William Thomas, who as a white boy had been adopted by the Cherokee Chief Yonaguska, convinced Tsali to turn himself over to the United States Government. The government agreed to pardon the remaining Indians hiding out in the mountains in exchange for Tsali's execution. Tsali gave himself up with the agreement that his sentence be carried out by his Cherokee brothers. Upon his death, the remaining Cherokee were allowed to return to their homeland. Although their land was much smaller and their numbers were greatly reduced, the Cherokee retained their mountain birthplace because of Tsali's sacrifice.

Later, as business chief of the Cherokee, Thomas was able to represent the Indians in land claims. He was a strong advocate in Congress for the rights of the Cherokee and had great influence on the establishment of the Qualla Boundary. In gratitude to Thomas, the Cherokee followed him into combat, fighting on the side of the Confederacy at the Battle of Deep Creek.

The fifty-six-thousand-acre Qualla Boundary is located at the southern end of the Blue Ridge Parkway. The Great Smoky Mountains National Park forms the reservation's northern boundary. Covering parts of five North Carolina counties, the Qualla Boundary is home to the communities of Yellowhill, Birdtown, Painttown, Snowbird, Big Cove, and Wolftown. Government affairs are carried out by a twelve-member Tribal Council, a Principal Chief, a Vice-Chief, and a number of Tribal departments.

A visit to Cherokee, capital of the Eastern Band of the Cherokee Nation, offers numerous opportunities to learn about the native Ameri-

The pioneer farm exhibit at the Great Smoky's Oconoluftee Visitor Center is one of many area attractions. Photo by Frank Logue.

cans who first inhabited the mountains and valleys of the Great Smokies. The lives of Sequoyah and other historical figures can be explored at the Museum of the Cherokee Indian located on US 441 at Drama Road. Visitors can watch audio-visual displays and view a priceless collection of artifacts. At the Cherokee Cyclorama Museum, which is three-fourths of a mile north of Cherokee on US 19, the story of the Cherokee is told through dioramas and taped lectures.

Since 1950, *Unto These Hills*, a live drama, has vividly portrayed the saga of the Cherokee struggle. The play brings North Carolina history alive, from Hernando de Soto's arrival in 1540 through the removal of the Cherokee in 1839. The two-hour production is performed each summer in a beautiful outdoor theater.

The Cherokee continue to preserve their culture through their traditional crafts. From mid May through October, visitors can see Cherokee artisans at work at the Oconaluftee Indian Village, a recreated Cherokee village of two hundred years ago. Maintained by the Cherokee Historical Association, this full-size replica village has demonstrations of all the Cherokee arts such as canoe-making, pottery, beading, weaving, and chipping flint for arrowheads. Qualla Arts and Crafts offers many of these remarkable hand-crafted wares for sale. It is recognized as the most outstanding Indian-owned and operated crafts cooperative in the United States.

Cherokee is a town that owes its existence to the tourist industry. With that in mind, expect to find the usual trappings of tourism. Despite the crowds, summer traffic, and trinket shops lining the main road, it is possible to "get back to nature." There is plenty of camping—over twenty-two hundred campsites in twenty-nine campgrounds. Many of the sites are along the Oconaluftee River. The Cherokee KOA has thirty-five acres with 420 sites from primitive to full hook-ups. They also have cabins.

For anglers, this is paradise. The Cherokee manage thirty miles of regularly stocked trout streams and six acres of ponds designated as "Enterprise Waters." More than two dozen local businesses offer daily tribal fishing permits.

Rent an inner-tube or fun-yak for a ride on the Oconaluftee River. Take a day trip into the Great Smoky Mountains National Park—just minutes away. The Cherokee Visitors Center, in the center of town, is the place to go for information on these activities and more.

As we hike the trails to the waterfalls near Cherokee, we feel the presence of Indians who must have used these same trails as footpaths in days-gone-by. The spirit of the Cherokee people dwells in the forests and mountains as certainly as the legendary "Little People" who live there still. We wonder if the Indians were as captivated by the falling waters as we are.

Little Creek Falls

4 miles roundtrip, Moderate

As with many things in life, there is a direct correlation between effort and reward. Little Creek Falls is no exception. You may be slightly winded or have tired legs from climbing the steep switchbacks by the time you get to the falls, but following the winding trail over streams and through dense rhododendron thickets is half the fun.

Little Creek cascades down hundreds of small sandstone shelves for a total height of ninety-five feet. The rock staircase magnifies the volume of the relatively small mountain stream as water dances from shelf to shelf. At the base of the falls there is a small pool and a natural (but slippery) bridge formed by logs and assorted debris. Standing on the bridge, you can almost reach out and touch the falls.

The trail crosses Little Creek three times, but some creative rock-hopping will keep your feet dry. A hundred yards after the first stream crossing, where Little Creek runs into Cooper Creek, the trail forks. There are no trail markers so be sure to go left. (Some kind-hearted soul placed sticks on the ground in the shape of an arrow. We didn't notice them until after we had mistakenly taken the right fork, which leads you away from the falls.)

The trail becomes steeper as you climb Thomas Ridge for one mile. After two more creek crossings and several switchbacks, the sound of rushing water tells you the falls are just around the bend. From the far side of the pool at the base, the trail continues for 0.2 miles to the top of the falls.

Directions: From Cherokee, take US 19 south to its intersection with US 441. Continue 5.8 miles to the community of Ela. Turn right at the Cooper Creek General Store and follow Cooper Creek Road for 3.4 miles. It ends on private property at a trout farm. Ask permission to park if possible, and if you park behind the horse barn, be careful not to block the gate. Walk 0.5 miles up the road to the trailhead on the left just before crossing the creek.

Waterfalls on Pigeon Creek Trail

Mingo Falls: 0.5 miles roundtrip, Moderate
Upper Mingo Falls: 1 mile roundtrip, Strenuous

Literature for Great Smoky Mountains National Park describes Mingo Falls as a "must see" for vacationers—even though it is not part of the Park! The reason? Mingo Falls is a most impressive sight. Although

Mingo Falls is one of the highest waterfalls in the area, dropping 120 feet, this is not the only feature that sets it apart from other falls. The water seems to fall in slow motion. This surreal effect is created by the stratified sandstone ledges—hundreds of tiny stair-steps in the rock face that slow the water.

Upper Mingo Falls is not mentioned in the Park's literature; and although there is a well-defined path, many people don't know about this hidden treasure. To unexpectedly discover Upper Mingo Falls is like finding money in an old jacket, a very pleasant surprise. Tucked away in a cove and shaded by rhododendrons, Upper Mingo Falls cascades twenty-five feet over beautiful, moss-covered rock.

The Pigeon Creek Trail is within the Qualla Indian Reservation. The first several hundred yards are steep, then the trail levels off to the base of Mingo Falls. To reach the top of Mingo Falls and Upper Mingo Falls, take the left fork off the main trail before getting to the base of the falls, ascend two switchbacks, climb a hill, and continue straight ahead. When the trail forks again, go right for a glimpse of the middle cascade of Mingo Falls or go left and climb the natural steps in a rock face to the top of Mingo Falls. The shaded trail to Upper Mingo Falls follows Mingo Creek back into the woods.

Directions: From Cherokee, go north on US 441 to Big Cove Road. Follow it for 5 miles. Mingo Falls Campground is on the right, 1 mile past the KOA Campground. Mingo Falls Campground is tribal property and non-campground users are welcome to park in the designated area. Pigeon Creek Trail begins behind the campground water system.

Flat Creek Falls

1.5 miles roundtrip, Moderate

Most waterfall hikes culminate at the base of the falls where you can sit and watch the play of water. That's what we were expecting when we visited Flat Creek Falls, and we were a little disappointed to find that you can't see the falls from the trail. Hiking to Flat Creek Falls was like spending time and effort in unwrapping an elaborate package, only to find the box empty. The gift, though, was really the wrapping–the pleasure of the hike.

Rushing water serenades you as you follow Bunches Creek just east of Heintooga Bald in the Balsam Mountains. The conifer forest, similar to that found in central Canada, is a reminder of the high elevation, approximately 3,400 feet. At the highest point along the trail, you have a grand view of Balsam Mountain Ridge and the surrounding valley. You'll find an unusual hardwood tree after the second log bridge. It is huge and hollow–three of us fit into the cavernous trunk for a family photo.

When you near the top of the falls, a warning sign directs you right to a spur trail ending at the lip of the falls. It appears the trail continues to the left of the sign but the abrupt drop and lack of view are good reasons to heed the suggestion to stop. Although Flat Creek disappears over the precipice, you have a great view of the creek looking upstream.

The best view of the falls is from Balsam Mountain Road, which runs along Heintooga Ridge near Wolf Laurel Gap. This is a good place to pull over and get out your binoculars. You will definitely need them because the falls is barely visible as Flat Creek plunges two hundred feet down the distant mountain ridge. Flat Creek Falls is one of the highest waterfalls in the Great Smoky Mountains National Park.

Directions: From Cherokee, head north on US 441 and pick up the Blue Ridge Parkway (turn right) before the entrance to Great Smoky Mountains National Park. Travel 11.1 miles and turn left onto Balsam Mountain Road. After 4.6 miles, pull over on the shoulder on the left for your best view of the falls. Then continue 0.8 miles to the trailhead on the left. (In the winter, be sure to check road conditions at the Oconaluftee Visitor Center, 0.8 miles up US 441 past the entrance to the Parkway.)

Soco Falls

0.1 miles roundtrip, Strenuous

Soco Falls is a dichotomy, God's splendor and man's trash. Unfortunately, the area around the pull-off and trail has become a convenient dumping ground. The nature lover's creed "take only memories, leave only footprints" was never more applicable.

Is Soco Falls worth a visit? Yes! And bring an empty trash bag. While it is sad to witness one of nature's wonders fouled by man's disregard, it reminds us that the preservation of beauty is the responsibility of those who treasure it.

Soco Creek and a larger unnamed creek weave their way through Soco Gorge and converge at right angles just south of Soco Gap to form an unusual sixty-foot, double-cascade called Soco Falls. As you face the falls, you'll notice Soco Creek entering from the left while the main cascade emerges from the shade, high above you. Leaping into full view, the water reflects the rays of the mid-day sun, creating a sparkling spectacle. The two creeks meet midway in their descent to the pool at the base of the falls. Soco Creek then flows down Soco Mountain into the Oconaluftee River in the town of Cherokee.

From the trailhead, you can hear the falls and a steep descent brings you to an overlook that provides a good view. Going to the base of the falls is not recommended because it involves climbing down a near-vertical embankment.

Soco is derived from the Cherokee word "Sog-wag" meaning "one." Legend links the name to Hernando DeSoto, the Spanish explorer. Supposedly, the Indians shouted "Soco" as they threw one of DeSoto's soldiers over the falls to his death (perhaps for littering?).

Soco Gap, the junction of US 19 and the Blue Ridge Parkway, marks the boundary of the Qualla Reservation of the Cherokee Indian. This was the initial point of the 1876 U.S. survey that created the reservation. Soco Gap is also referred to as "ambush place," where the Cherokees wiped out a raiding party of Iroquois Indians.

Directions: From the Visitor's Center in Cherokee, travel 10.6 miles north on US 19. There is a small pull-off, accommodating three or four cars, on the right side of the road. There are no signs, but the graffiti on the guardrail marks the spot. The trailhead is at the upper end of the guardrail.

22

Bryson City

Bryson City lies within Swain County, where eighty-six percent of the land is owned by the federal government. Tourists are drawn here by the bountiful natural resources the county has to offer. They come for the mountains; forty percent of the Great Smoky Mountain National Park is in Swain County and includes Clingman's Dome, the king of the mountains. They come for the waters; Swain County has four rivers—the Nantahala, the Tuckaseigee, the Little Tennessee, and the Oconaluftee—and one lake, the beautiful Fontana Lake. And they come for the forests; part of the 517,436-acre Nantahala National Forest lies within Swain County. The county itself is small, with only about sixty thousand acres, but more people visit Swain County than any other area of North Carolina.

The land that includes present-day Bryson City was first owned and inhabited by Cherokee Chief Big Bear. Under an 1817 treaty between the U.S. Government and the Cherokee Indians, Chief Big Bear received 640 acres (one mile square) on the Tuckaseigee River. This included the Indian village of Younaahqua (or Big Bear Springs) and the land west of the mouth of Deep Creek.

Chief Big Bear later sold a portion of his reserve to John B. Love, supposedly for two white horses and a rig. The land had several other owners over the years. One of these owners was Alfred Cline, whose

The Nantahala Gorge attracts kayakers and rafters to the "Land of the Noonday Sun." Photo by Frank Logue.

widow, Lucy, donated twenty-five acres in 1873 for the town square of the county seat, Charleston.

Colonel Thaddeus Dillard Bryson bought a large tract of the land on the north side of the Tuckaseigee River. Bryson built a home and operated a grist mill at the mouth of Deep Creek. In 1889, the county seat of Charleston was renamed Bryson City in honor of Thaddeus, who was the first to represent Swain County in the North Carolina State Legislature.

The "Iron Horse" came to Bryson City in 1884, and with it came a new way of life. Industry followed the railroad. The densely forested land and abundance of water made this prime timber property; logging became the backbone of the county's economy.

The railroad followed the Tuckaseigee from the town of Sylva; the construction took a tremendous amount of manpower and convict labor was often used. During the building of the railway's Cowee Tunnel, a flatboat carrying convict workers across the Tuckaseigee capsized in the swift waters of the river. Nineteen convicts, shackled together at the ankles, drowned in the icy current. The men are buried in an unmarked grave on a nearby hillside, and their ghosts are said to haunt the tunnel.

In spite of the perils involved in its construction, the railroad proved to be a boon to Bryson City. It brought in tourists from the lowlands and took freight to distant markets. The numerous logging operations depended on the railroad for their survival, and the mountain folk depended on the logging operations for a steady paycheck.

When the Great Smoky Mountains National Park was formed in the 1930s, logging ceased entirely, but the railroad remained. In earlier times, the railroad was the only mode of transportation between communities; today the "Scenic Line" of the Great Smoky Mountains Railway is a popular tourist attraction. The Railway offers a number of roundtrip excursions through this beautiful section of western North Carolina. The marvelous views of the Smokies and the nostalgic allure of the railroad combine to provide a magnificent trip.

The Nantahala Gorge Excursion begins at the Bryson City Depot, a turn-of-the-century railway station that has been restored, and takes you through the spectacular Nantahala Gorge. The train crosses a 791-foot trestle over blue-green Fontana Lake, known as "the Jewel of the Smokies."

From a height of 179 feet, passengers can look down on the sparkling waters of Fontana; at thirty-one miles long, this is one of the largest lakes in the Appalachians. It was created in the 1940s when TVA built the massive Fontana Dam, which at 480 feet is the highest dam in eastern America. You can take a tram inside the dam for a tour of the turbine room and a film on the building of the dam. (But that is for another day.)

The train runs parallel to the Nantahala River, which flows through the picturesque Nantahala Gorge. Nantahala, the Cherokee word meaning "Land of the Noonday Sun," aptly describes this deep and narrow gorge. The Nantahala River flows through the eight-mile gorge and lies in mysterious shadow except when the sun is directly overhead.

Passengers watch and wave to the hundreds of folks in whitewater rafts, kayaks, and canoes on the river. After witnessing their delight, you will want to add a rafting adventure to your list of fun things to do while in Bryson City. There are several companies that provide raft rentals. One outfitter, Wildwater Ltd., offers a ride on the railroad and a ride on the river for one price on their "Raft & Rail" excursion.

The trail stops at the Nantahala Outdoor Center, where passengers can spend some time before the return trip to Bryson City. In operation for over twenty years, NOC is one of the premier outfitters in the world. This unique combination inn, restaurant, and outdoor center offers whitewater thrills and instruction at all levels. The expert staff includes several whitewater national champions.

In addition to raft trips and whitewater kayak and canoe instruction, NOC offers rock climbing courses and mountain biking tours, as well as corporate programs and ropes courses. NOC's Adventure Travel Program sponsors trips throughout the country and all over the world— places such as Nepal, Costa Rica, New Zealand, Alaska, Mexico, Scotland, and the Grand Canyon of the Colorado River.

Before the train departs, try Relia's Garden Restaurant. The delicious fare includes fresh ingredients from the gardens out front. Our daughters were impressed with the edible flowers in the beautifully prepared salad. The restaurant is run by Aurelia Kennedy who, along with her husband Payson, is one of the "originals" at NOC.

While it is wonderful to experience the splendor of this area from the comfort of a railway car, the only way to explore the magic of the mountains is to walk in them. Three miles north of Bryson City in the Great Smoky Mountains National Park, Deep Creek Campground offers the opportunity to experience the woodlands "feet-first" on the trails in the basin of Deep Creek. This developed campground has over one hundred sites for tents or RVs, plus water, flush toilets, and picnic areas. From here, you can explore virgin forest and even arrange for the ranger to take you on a night walk.

This was Horace Kephart territory. The environmentalist, who was so instrumental in the Park's formation, had a permanent camp called Bryson Place on Deep Creek. He wrote of the area, "I lived for several years in the heart of it...always vital, growing new shapes of beauty from day to day."

The expropriation of Swain County for the Great Smoky Mountains National Park, Fontana Lake, and the Nantahala National Forest took away three-fourths of its taxable land, destroying the lumber industry and almost devastating the county financially. Ironically, the things that almost destroyed the county have become its greatest assets.

The Constitution of the State of North Carolina contains an emphatic statement about protecting the state's land and waters for the benefit of its citizens. Because the people of Swain County overcame temporary adversity for the long-term benefit of preservation, visitors to this mountain paradise can enjoy its land and waters, following forest paths and mountain streams to the waterfalls around Bryson City.

Juneywhank Falls

0.5 miles roundtrip, Easy

When you stand on the log bridge that crosses Juneywhank Falls, you are surrounded by the sights and sounds of rushing water. The eighty-foot cascade that begins above you, runs under your feet, and descends below you on its way to the valley floor to join Deep Creek. You have a spectacular view of the falls, as well as the forest with its abundant laurel, rhododendron, and holly.

The eight-inch wide bridge has handrails and is easy to traverse, but the look on the face of our terrified eight year-old daughter Cory, would not have confirmed this. "I'm not going across that bridge and you can't make me!" After some persistent encouragement, she succeeded and felt good about her accomplishment. Walking over a waterfall on a log bridge is quite an adventure for a kid and makes for good story-telling back at school.

Juneywhank Falls has an unusual name; it was probably named for a local resident, Junaluska Whank. Called Juney by his friends, he was named after the famous Cherokee Chief Junaluska. Legend has it that Whank is buried close to the falls.

Directions: Leave Bryson City from the train depot, which is on the

An eight-inch wide log bridge crosses Juneywhank Falls. Photo by John Newman.

corner of Depot and Everett. Turn right (heading east) onto Depot Street and travel 4 miles to Deep Creek Campground. Depot Street will become West Deep Creek Road. You will find the main parking area 0.5 miles from the entrance. Walk a couple of hundred yards back (along the road just traveled) to the trail marker on the right.

Waterfalls on Deep Creek Trail

Toms Branch Falls: 0.4 miles roundtrip, Easy
Indian Creek Falls: 2 miles roundtrip, Easy

It would be hard to find a hike that offers more scenery and adventure than Deep Creek Trail. You can walk along the creek and view two beautiful waterfalls, then you can ride the rollicking waters on an inner-tube back to your car.

During the summer, inner-tubes can be rented at the campground entrance. Adventurous tubers put in 0.75 miles up the trail from the parking lot, while youngsters and first-timers start at the 0.5-mile mark. Whichever stretch you choose, repeat rides can provide a full day's entertainment. If you want to be a spectator, you can watch the fun from the foot bridge over Deep Creek.

The trail is a wide abandoned roadway with a mild slope. Kids won't notice the grade; however, at the end of a day of tubing, their parents might.

Toms Branch pours into Deep Creek over eighty feet of stratified sandstone forming Toms Branch Falls. These sparse but spirited waters shift left, right, and then left again as the cascade tumbles over seven multi-tiered ledges. Although the majority of hikers would not require a rest this early on the trail, there is a bench opposite the falls that provides an ideal spot to sit and ponder this delightful example of Mother Nature's handiwork.

Indian Creek Falls is a high-volume cascade—noisy and boisterous—that plunges twenty-five feet into a large inviting pool at the base. The main flow is on the left, with two smaller cascades on the right partially hidden by rhododendron and other vegetation. Another trail-side bench provides a place to enjoy the sights and sounds of rushing water. And, you can hike down the spur trail for a closer view.

Directions: Leave Bryson City and travel to Deep Creek Campground (see directions under Juneywhank Falls). The trailhead is at the upper end of the main parking lot.

White Oak Falls
and Camp Branch Falls

No hike necessary

In the 12,076-acre Southern Nantahala Wilderness Area, part of the Nantahala National Forest, there are two easy-access, roadside waterfalls. A drive up to White Oak Falls and Camp Branch Falls makes a perfect ending to a day of rafting on the Nantahala River.

White Oak Falls is a high-volume cascade that plummets over a granite face, a free-fall of forty feet. Two hundred yards after the falls, White Oak Creek joins the Nantahala River. Although you can view the falls from your car, stretch your legs awhile and rock hop to the base of the falls or walk the paved road to see the falls from the top. Many of the local rafting employees find the sun-drenched rocks make a perfect spot to "while away" the hours, read, eat lunch, of just "veg out."

Sources at the Nantahala Outdoor Center verify that White Oak Falls has been run successfully by highly skilled kayakers. Despite the apparent absence of a clear route and the suicidal drop into a shallow rocky pool, there is a narrow line that can be negotiated if run perfectly. It looks impossible. I was told that the boaters who accomplished this feat were "true experts...if not slightly demented."

Camp Branch Falls is best viewed as you drive back down the mountain from White Oak Falls. Flowing through the Burning Town Area, Camp Branch Creek begins its descent from a mountain ridge as a narrow chute of water and quickly fans out. Dropping 150 feet over a series of ledges, Camp Branch Falls flows into the Nantahala River.

At least two famous travelers passed through the Nantanhala Lake area. A Cherokee peace chief known as Atakullakulla (Little Carpenter) was said to have met the American botanist William Bartram here. The botanist traveled through Georgia, Florida, North and South Carolina, Alabama, and Louisana between 1773 and 1776 studying and drawing the area's diverse plants and animals.

Directions: Leave Bryson City, heading south on US 19 for approximately 13 miles to the Nantahala Gorge. After passing the Nantahala Outdoor Center on the right, continue south for another 8 miles, along the Nantahala River. Turn left onto Put-in Road (NC 1310) at the public landing for whitewater boaters. For White Oak Falls, drive 4 miles (until you see the waterfall), turn onto FS 308, and pull off on the shoulder. For Camp Branch Falls, head back down the mountain for 1.3 miles and pull off on the right side of the road.

Appendix A—Important Addresses

Asheville Travel
and Tourism
P.O. Box 1010
Asheville, NC 28802-1010
704-258-3858

Blowing Rock Chamber
of Commerce
P.O. Box 406
Blowing Rock, NC 28605
704-295-7851

Blue Ridge Parkway
Superintendent
700 Northwestern Plaza
Asheville, NC 28801
704-259-0769

Brevard Chamber of
Commerce
P.O. Box 589
Brevard, NC 28712
704-883-3700

Bryson City
Swain County Chamber
of Commerce
P.O. Box 509-T
Bryson City, NC 28713
704-488-3681 (ext. T)

Cashiers Welcomes You
Box 238-Y
Cashiers, NC 28717
704-743-5191

Cherokee Chamber of
Commerce
P.O. Box 465-56
Cherokee, NC 28719
704-497-9195

Clifton Forge
Alleghany Highlands
Chamber of Commerce
403 East Ridgeway Street
Clifton Forge, VA 24422
703-862-4969

George Washington
National Forest
P.O. Box 233
Harrisonburg, VA 22801
(703) 433-2491

Glasgow
Lexington Visitor Center
102 East Washington Street
Lexington, VA 24450
703-463-3777

Great Smokies National Park
Headquarters Office
Gatlinburg, TN 37738
615-436-6516

Hanging Rock State Park
P.O. Box 186
Danbury, NC 27016
919-593-8480

Highlands Chamber of Commerce
P.O. Box 404
Highlands, NC 28741
704-525-2112

Jefferson National Forest
210 Franklin Road SW
Roanoke, VA 24001
(703) 982-6270

Lake Toxaway
Brevard Chamber of Commerce
P.O. Box 589
Brevard, NC 28712
704-883-3700

Linville
Avery County Chamber
of Commerce
P.O. Box 700
Newland, NC 28657
704-733-4737

Little Switzerland
McDowell County
Chamber of Commerce
17 North Garden Street
Marion, NC 28752
704-652-4240

Luray
Page County Chamber
of Commerce
46 East Main Street
Luray, VA 22835
703-743-3915

Marion
McDowell County
Chamber of Commerce
17 North Garden Street
Marion, NC 28752
704-652-4240

Pisgah Forest
US Forest Service
P.O. Box 8
Pisgah Forest, NC 28768
704-877-3265

Shenandoah National Park
Superintendent
Luray, VA 22835
703-999-2266

South Mountains State Park
Route 1, Box 206-C
Connelly Springs, NC 28612
704-433-4772

Stone Mountain State Park
Star Route 1, Box 17
Roaring Gap, NC 28668
919-957-8185

Waynesboro
East Augusta Chamber
of Commerce
301 West Main Street
Waynesboro, VA 22980
703-949-8203

Appendix B—Bibliography

Albright, Rodney and Priscilla. *Walks in the Great Smokies.* Chester, CT: Globe Pequot Press, 1990.

Adkins, Leonard M. *Walking the Blue Ridge.* Chapel Hill, NC: The University of North Carolina Press, 1991.

Biggs Jr., Walter C. and James F. Parnell. *State Parks of North Carolina.* Winston-Salem, NC: John F. Blair, Publisher, 1989.

Boyd, Brian. *Waterfalls of the Southern Appalachians.* Conyers, GA: Ferncreek Press, 1990.

Bryson City Genealogical and Historical Society. *100 Years of Progress.* Bryson City, NC: Chamber of Commerce, 1989.

Cantu, Rita. *Great Smoky Mountains: The Story Behind the Scenery.* Las Vegas, NV: KC Publications, 1979.

Catlin, David T. *A Naturalist's Blue Ridge Parkway.* Knoxville, TN: University of Tennessee Press, 1984.

Colbert, Judy and Ed. *Virginia: Off the Beaten Path.* Chester, CT: Globe Pequot Press, 1986, 1989.

Corey, Jane. *Exploring the Waterfalls of North Carolina.* Chapel Hill, NC: The Provincial Press, 1991.

Crandall, Hugh. *Shenandoah: The Story Behind the Scenery.* Las Vegas, NV: KC Publications, 1990.

de Hart, Allen. *North Carolina Hiking Trails.* Boston, MA: Appalachian Mountain Club Books, 1988.

Frome, Michael. *Strangers in High Places.* New York, NY: Double-day and Company, 1966.

Hampton, Bruce, and David Cole. *Soft Paths.* Harrisburg, PA: Stackpole Books, 1988.

Hanson, Peggy, and Frances Pledger. *Touring Transylvania.* Brevard, NC: Highland Publishing, 1986.

Hubbs, Hal, Charles Maynard, and David Morris. *Waterfalls and Cascades of the Great Smoky Mountains.* Seymour, TN: Panther Press, 1992.

Jolley, Harley E. *The Blue Ridge Parkway.* Knoxville, TN: University of Tennessee Press, 1969.

Johnson, Randy. *The Hiker's Guide to Virginia.* Helena and Billings, MT: Falcon Press, 1992.

McIntosh, Gert. *Highlands, North Carolina. A Walk into the Past.* Highlands, NC: By the author, 1983.

Morrison, Mark. *Waterfalls Walks and Drives of Northeast Georgia and the Western Carolinas.* Douglasville, GA: H.F. Publishing, 1992.

Pitzer, Sara. *North Carolina: Off the Beaten Path.* Chester, CT: Globe Pequot Press, 1990.

Plemmons, Jan C. *Treasures of Toxaway.* Jacksonville, FL: By the author, 1984.

Potomac Appalachian Trail Club. *Appalachian Trail Guide to Shenandoah National Park.* Vienna, VA: By the author, 1986.

Roe, Charles E. *North Carolina Wildlife Viewing Guide*. Helena and Billings, MT: Falcon Press Publishing Company, 1992.

Shoemaker, Michael T. *Hiking Guide to the Pedlar District: George Washington National Forest*. Washington, DC: Potomac Appalachian Trail Club, 1990.

Tinsley, Jim Bob. *The Land of the Waterfalls: Transylvania County, North Carolina*. Brevard, NC: J.B. Tinsley and Dottie Tinsley, 1988.

Valentine, James. *North Carolina*. Portland, OR: Graphic Arts Center, 1990.

Wenberg, Donald C. *Blue Ridge Mountain Pleasures*. Chester, CT: Globe Pequot Press, 1988.

Index

Colophon

The text of this book was set in a digital version of Goudy Old Style. The typeface was created by Frederic Goudy in 1915 for American Type Founders. The display type is set in ITC Souvenir italic. The book was designed and composed by Frank Logue of Carolina Graphics Group in Rome, Georgia.

The cover photo was taken by Joe Cook. The inset photo of Raven Fork Falls was taken by Ben Keys. The cover design is by Leslie Cummins.

Printed and bound by Alabama Press Printing & Litho
in Birmingham, Alabama